ECODEVELOPMENT

To Anna and Kate

That man's physical and spiritual life is linked to
nature means simply that nature is linked to itself,
for man is part of nature.

Karl Marx

The Economic and Philosophic Manuscripts of 1844

ECODEVELOPMENT

**Economics, Ecology and Development
An Alternative to Growth Imperative Models**

Robert Riddell

St. Martin's Press   New York

Library of Congress Cataloging in Publication Data

Riddell, Robert, 1934–

  Ecodevelopment: economics, ecology and development

  Bibliography: p.
  1. Environmental policy. 2. Economic development – –
  Environmental aspects. I. Title.

  HC79.E5R52   338.9   80-21312
  ISBN 0-312-22585-7

ISBN 0-312-22585-7

Contents

Diagrams

Tables

Preface

The question this text addresses runs: What is the form and content of a development model which is economically equitable, socially ennobling and environmentally balanced? This must at once beg the further question, in the minds of those already active in development planning theory, as to why the models they espouse are not seen to meet these requirements. Simply stated, underdevelopment in Southern, low income countries is linked economically and environmentally to overdevelopment in Northern, higher income countries; and the international arrangements in operation during the last two 'development decades' have, if anything, strengthened the already strong and privileged whilst eroding the already weak and deprived. Some countries have increased their resource exploitation as a result of planning with conventional development models; but population expansion, currency devaluations, resource depletions and a brutalisation of their habitat have, on balance, resulted in reduced *per capita* material standards.

Conventional development models delude low income countries on two major counts. First, they hold out material improvements attained through economic growth based upon the expropriation of resources and the exploitation of labour; second, the poor majority in these countries, and their political champions, are mollified by antidotal aid 'given' to combat disease, disaster and illiteracy. External involvement in development for low income nations is more concerned with maintaining flows of resources that are non-existent or running out at home, and obtaining the strategic security of partnership at world fora or, ultimately, on the battlefield. The 'improved' society held out by the Northern nations as a reward for this allegience is, broadly speaking, an implied version of either the Northern capitalist or the Northern socialist society—both, in essence, consumer societies. The font of life for such consumer societies is growth; but growth in the original versions was necessarily based, among other things, on inequality within and between Nations. Who, then can these poor nations now exploit for their own growth but themselves, creating in the process the selfsame dividend society which independence from colonialism was to absolve. The pages of history are littered with economically imperialist civilisations which degraded their own resources, pushed their frontiers too far and fell into bureaucratic disorder. Similarly, modern consumer societies exist in and for themselves, and in order to maintain their rate of consumption they are bound to be parasitic, for they owe their wealth to the enforced use of unequal exchange as an institution of exclusion in trade and government. There is no way that low income nations can benefit, in aggregate, from this approach; and those middle income nations that have decided to try and establish consumer growth institutions must be warned to look carefully to their resource utilisation policies in order to strike balanced exchanges.

The real point here is that economic systems which score success according to gross national product *per capita* are largely irrelevant, both as measures of worth and as ladders to improvement, particularly in relation to poorer populations struggling to exist within near-subsistence, natural economies. Their lot is hard, but it is not improved by models that are only able to record gains in a manner whereby local resources are turned, through third party consumption, into cash flows that are a surrogate for the real wealth expropriated abroad. Apart from being socially undesirable because it is heavily skewed towards the economically elite, this form of cash flow begets many another neo-Malthusian mischief, not the least being an unfavourable change in the human eco-system as non-renewable resources are stripped, the productivity of renewable resources are impaired, populations grow to a point where the sustainable ratio of people to land is put under stress, and the habitats of communities are dehumanised through overcrowding and pollution. A price has to be paid—there is, alas, no free lunch—nor is there anything really sustainable as a technological fix. Indeed, inappropriate technology acquired from the profits of resource expropriation does more to handicap than help low income nations. Thus, have higher yielding varieties of rice, maize and wheat with their vast outputs per hectare, but lower protein per unit of weight, been any real help to malnourished nations? Have not curative and preventative health programmes, administered without birth limitation as a concomitant part of the package, induced a pathological population crisis? Can it be denied that mass education with its high absorption of skilled labour into teaching and low employment at the end of the line, fuels discontent?

Turning now to ecological systems, the central issue is energy: the exploitation of energy sources, energy conversion and power generation.

The 'soft' energy options, such as harnessing solar power, hydro-potential and vegetable alcohol production generate no insoluble problems; but 'hard' energy options involving a reliance upon fossil fuels and uranium can, on the one hand, lead to short term benefits whilst, on the other, they store up great difficulties in energy supply for the future. Whilst this point is usually acknowledged, it is difficult for any individual to see how his or her energy conservation practice can help. Fossil fuels are utilised very largely in accordance with the creed for exploiting 'free' goods. Thus, if one person foregoes access, others will optimise their consumption and the conservationist will merely end up empty handed and cynical. Difficulties over energy policy are particularly acute for Northern nations, but poorer countries with large populations must see that hard energy technologies lead to a dead end because, even if the nuclear solution materialises, it will not be the one they can afford.

From a global perspective, the significant world is really only a grain within the solar system. And on our globe, the lithosphere, from which mankind draws sustenance, is about in proportion to the thin outer skin of an onion; and the living parts within that lithosphere are limited in extent, patchy and fragile. Of course, solar energy is arriving constantly and can, along with its hydro, tidal and wind offshoots, be relied upon. But the fuel stored in oil, coal and uranium reserves is absorbing more and more energy per unit of useful output gained and once all the energy expended in extracting and converting these mineral fuel resources is used up, that's it; for the dissipation of energy from stored sources is available to mankind only once in the history of human civilisations. In the present context, this understanding of resource limits must be linked with our knowledge of the fragility of a biosphere where deforestation, soil exhaustion, fish exploitation and widespread oceanic and atmospheric pollution is clearly shrinking the surface area available to sustain human life. In short, the development models which have reinforced the Northern thrust for economic growth at home cannot be extrapolated from known planetary resources for the global population.

Is it the case that the low income Southern nations are not up to the task before them? Has colonialism emasculated their economies and totally undermined confidence? Is it necessary to wait until matters reach crisis point before there is a reaction? The answer is 'no' on all counts—but there are many complexities to consider. These have little to do with flows of cash from the rich. Nor have they to do with disadvantaged resource endowments being, somehow, magically transformed by a technological fix. The greatest difficulty debarring fulfilment of the goals of ecodevelopment are organisational; and here new nations have to overcome, politically, the awful legacies of colonial fervour; resource exploitation, fossil fuel capitalism and missionary zeal. Authoritarian rule, officialism and technical controls placed in the hands of persons not subject to election can lead nations away from the point of independence, independence itself; a retreat from empathy and democracy within a country and an inroad for control from without.

Ethical beliefs and moral values, ideals, are seen to constitute the most dynamic force in the past—and for the future. From the past we can locate co-operative ideals and collective beliefs which align with modern ecodevelopment, and wait to be rediscovered. A step backwards? Has the 'individualism' of the Protestant ethic or the international ambitions of Western communism been such a great step towards balance? Somewhat tentatively, for there are at least as many sets of beliefs in the world as there are languages, my call would be to seek a co-operative cultural sympathy for the ecodevelopment philosophy. The underlying reasoning is that for low income nations theistic beliefs, particularly Christianity, are associated with capitalism, ending up in exploitation for many and riches for a privileged few; and atheism, broadly equated with communism, ends up in frugal socialism for many and, similarly, as riches for a privileged few. Co-operative culturalism, more dramatically depicted as pantheism, is territorially discreet, is against resource depletion and waste, advocates a balance between man and land, offers a rational, humanitarian and democratic foundation for smaller government and provides an environmentally balanced basis for development that can be culturally identified with the pre-colonial past.

The foregoing has attempted to explain why an 'alternative' attitude to development—concerned more with regional human progress than national economic growth—is imperative for low income nations. The text that follows outlines the components for such an alternative— ecodevelopment: development leading to economic 'equity', social 'harmony' and environmental 'balance'. The practical policy components for ecodevelopment, witnessed from a low income viewpoint, occupy much of the book. In the first chapter, material policy points are made which touch upon such vital issues as poverty alleviation, disease eradication, self-reliance, urbanisation, renewable resource conservation, non-renewable resource exploitation and environmental protection. Part I, which follows this identification, serves as an introduction to the causal resources, ecosystems and human factors which point to the need for an alternative approach to development. The structural *desiderata* supporting the pursuit of such policies are set down in Part II where stress is laid upon administrative guidelines and linkages. As a development planner with experience at central, local and institutional levels of government, I appreciate the need to relate structural and organisational criteria to practical planning endeavour—this is discussed in Part III. Part IV is an overview in which emphasis is laid upon the need for a new internal order for low income nations.

The book which follows was written at Cambridge, it being a happy sabbatical opportunity that found me with the University of Papua New Guinea at Lae when this preface was called for. Holding onto ecological virtue at Cambridge is, on the one hand, difficult because of the inclination towards elitism and privilege; and on the other testing on account of the post-Keynsian aura that pervades the cloisters. But here in Papua New Guinea—mindful of the ideals of the Eight Point Development Plan*—the cultural and natural environment renders eco-development fundamentally imperative; for here local and exogenous entrepreneurs have combined to get at resources with awesome efficiency. Papua New Guinea is a newly independent country still economically and politically tied up, and it will take time before there is generative progress for all in line with the fine rhetoric of the Development Plan.

The acceptance of change is always problematic, but for any low income nation the association of development with territorially discreet units of organisation, which link historically and culturally to pre-colonial society, has popular appeal. Equally clear is the fact that where imitative development for 'economic growth' has failed by collective criteria, the generative ideal of 'human progress' underlying ecodevelopment is bound to prove beneficial to poorer societies; bled through feudalism and exploitation, there is really no other way for many of them to go—a perverse advantage for the present thesis.

A final question occupies me, although it is not the subject of the present text: whither the Northern nations? One hope is that although this book is concerned with low income regions, perhaps the notion of generative progress from within—which couples economic equity, social harmony and environmental balance into a composite development package—will, in the fullness of time rather than from the futility of war, come to be seen as apposite for both rich and poor nations alike.

* See Appendix

Acknowledgements

In a text which purports to express an alternative development strategy, it appears valid to commence my acknowledgement with a conventional disclaimer absolving those associated in any way with the work from responsibility for its arguments and hypotheses. Nevertheless, the progenitors of my thesis can be noted materially as the then Ministry of Overseas Development which, on the prompting of Professor (now Emeritus) D.R. Denman of Cambridge funded field enquiries from 1974 to 1976 concerned with the environmental dimension to development in low income countries: and conceptually, above all, by the mid 1970s writings of Brookfield (*Interdependent Development*, 1975) and Mishan (*The Economic Growth Debate*, 1976). As the text took shape, sections of it were put forward as Discussion Papers for seminars within the Cambridge Courses on Development; and the lively African, Asian and Latin American viewpoints given by the graduate Study Fellows did much to inform the manuscript. Some eighty students on the Lands Policy option joined these seminars from 1975–80, and it would be unfair to single out any particular names for mention. Outside the Development Studies Unit other friends offered useful critical comment as individuals. John Mathers and Jenny Brownson at Darwin College gave views on the environmental aspects of Chapters 2 and 3; Simon Collis, then an English undergraduate at Christ's College, commented helpfully upon style and lucidity at an early draft stage; my wife, Pam, at King's College, gave very valuable insights in discussion and in the rewriting of later drafts; and most of all I would like to thank Chris Pounder, now of Edinburgh University, who gave a lot of his time and put up a great number of political and philosophical markers throughout the text. These views from other disciplines and from people committed in different ways to an 'alternative' society were refreshing and extremely useful. A quartet of really good secretaries: Anne Madoc-Jones, Sarah Yates, Juliet Rigby and Fiona Moss assisted professionally with the referencing, typing and alterations to the manuscript, and they have my special thanks. Finally, I gratefully acknowledge an intellectual debt to colleagues for their stimulus and encouragement: John Cathie, Patrick Drudy, Mohammed Qadeer and my close colleague, Henry West. The debates continue.

Robert Riddell
Wolfson College, Cambridge
November 1980

Glossary

The aim with this glossary is to give understanding to terms which are not outlined in the text or which may not be given the definition intended within specialist dictionaries, of which good examples are:

A Dictionary of Geography by F.J. Monkhouse

Dictionary of Economic Terms by Alan Gilpin

The Environment: A Dictionary of the World About Us by Geoffrey Hollister and Andrew Porteous

Agribusiness
Large scaled organisation, production, processing, distribution and marketing of food and fibre commodities for profit.

Appropriate technology
Appropriate technology recognises that communities with differing social affinities and resource endowments can be served by a variety of technologies appropriate to their differing circumstances. 'Appropriateness' can vary greatly between consumer oriented and self-reliant societies: hence 'socially' appropriate (job generating and labour saving) and 'environmentally' appropriate (fossil energy saving and solar energy using) technologies.

Balance
A quantitative term. The induction of sustained yields by methods which maintain an equilibrium between the utilisation and regeneration of renewable resources.

Biomass
The weight of living matter on and within a given surface area. Biomass is usually expressed in terms of grammes per square metre. A distinction can be made between producers (plants) and consumers (animals, bacteria and fungi).

Black box

A part of a *system* about which nothing is known except the inputs and outputs: internally it is 'black'. Thus, to many, the combusion engine is a 'black box' within an automobile; petrol, air, oil and water are added as inputs and motion is the main output.

Carrying capacity
The population (human and animal) that can be sustained by an *ecosystem*. Carrying capacity is most readily understood when it is expressed in terms of 'standard stock units' (each unit being 500 kg live weight) of animal per square kilometre. Overpopulation occurs when carrying capacity is exceeded.

Conservation
The utilisation and maintenance of renewable resources in a manner which ensures that future production and purifying capacities are relatively unimpaired. See, also, the more circumscribed definition for *preservation*.

Cybernetics
Understanding the working of a *system* in order to control its behaviour by using servo-mechanical devices.

Desertification
The terrestrial extension of desert conditions leading to reduced production of *biomass* and an attendant lowering of *carrying capacity*.

Development
A relative term indicating quantitative change. Positive development occurs when a human social group moves toward a condition of life wherein the present is perceived overall as an improvement upon the past. Development is mainly expressed in monetary measures of value and may thus usefully represent comparability between economically advanced economies. See, also, *progress* for a representation of compatability for low income economies.

Ecodevelopment
Ecodevelopment induces desirable, *soft* change for a human social group, which is held to be not only better, but in economic (broadly social) and ecological equilibrium.

Ecosystem
A biotic community of plants and animals within an abiotic setting of water, minerals, atmosphere and climate.

Efficiency
A quantitative factor expressing the ratio of outputs over inputs. Thus 200 units of currency profit from an investment of 100 units on a hectare of agricultural land represents an economic efficiency factor of X 2. The same area of land might produce 4000 keal units of useful food from 1000 keal units of energy (other than solar) input, representing an energy efficiency factor of X 4. Care must be taken to define the units of measurement and the components that are to be included in the calculation.

Endogenous
Growing from within; appertaining to that which happens within a *system.*

Energy
A force capable of being harnessed in a productive way. There are two kinds of energy: kinetic, which is motive (solar, wind, tidal) and potential which is in store (fossil fuels, nuclear, chemical). The obscure and tiny joule (J) (the unit of energy produced from one ampre acting for one second against one ohm) is the internationally preferred basic unit. A megajoule (MJ) is J10, a much more useful unit.

1 kilowatt hour	=	3.6 MJ
1000 keals (nutritional calories)	=	4.19 MJ
1 litre of petrol	=	35.0 MJ
1 therm	=	105.5 MJ

Energy accounting
A particular aspect of *environmental impact analysis* which assesses the inputs and outputs of *energy* which are 'invested' and 'gained' from a project.

Entropy
The second law of thermo-dynamics (the 'entropic' law) states that all *systems* tend toward an end state of maximum disorder or entropy. Thus fuel is transformed in a combustion engine from a low entropy state (petrol) to a high entropy state of expended power, low grade heat and dispersed carbon molecules.

Environment
The physical setting within which an organism or a human social community exists.

Environmental impact analyses (EIA)
A scientific procedure which provides a diagnosis of the consequences of an environmental kind which can be expected to arise from a resource-using, urbanisation, industrial, transportation or military project. These

consequences are expressed in terms of monetary, energy, social and aesthetic quanta.

Equity
A qualitative concept, which defies rigorous definition, expressing the common, in addition to any statutory, understanding of rightness and appropriateness.

Exogenous
Inputs of an externally generated kind from without a *system*.

Exploitation
The action of turning a resource to account in accordance with profit motives and without regard to environmental consequences or any real concern for a regeneration of the resource.

Free goods
Goods theoretically available to all (for example, fresh air and delightful perspectives) but which are usually 'consumed' more by some than others.

Gross national product
One measure of aggregate economic activity—the total market value of finished goods and services. Disaggregated it is described as *per capita* product. A complication is that goods and services are expressed as gains with no debit for environmental pollution, social costs or (usually) capital depreciation.

Hard (development, technology, energy, etc.)
An approach to the solution of a problem or the exploitation of a potential which is sophisticated, capital intensive, urgent and relatively unconsequential.

Modernisation
A form of *development/progress* which arises from the use of *appropriate technology*; and which, at its best, includes growth in education, conservation of renewable resources, freedom of expression, social mobility, preservation of heritage, increases in social welfare and other socially desirable and environmentally adaptive components.

Normative
Planning in a style wherein the future is an extension of the present without great shifts in political or technological emphasis. The *status quo* is expected to continue.

Opportunity cost
The real cost involved in satisfying a want, including any opportunities foregone. For example, a private home built on a piece of land formerly used as a playground represents, in fulfilling the homebuilders' want, a foregoing of opportunities for children to play.

Planning
The rational application of human knowledge to the process of reaching decisions; in short, the establishment of relationships between means and ends with the object of achieving the latter by the most efficient use of the former.

Political ecology
An ideology synthesised from the social and natural sciences which is concerned primarily with the political and organisational problems involved in ecologically balancing human desires and needs.

Polluter pays principle (PPP)
Application of this principle requires that a polluter be charged with the cost of abatement. The principle is not violated when the originator recovers abatement costs earlier or later on in the price mechanism.

Pollution (pollutant)
A pollutant is an undesirable substance in the wrong place at the wrong time. Pollution is an undesirable material change in an *ecosystem* or *environment* caused by natural or human agents, whether deliberately or unintentionally induced.

Preservation
The maintenance of an *ecosystem* in a manner which ensures, through the restriction of human and other external influences, that the foreseeable future state of the ecosystem will be similar to the present state or will revert to a former unimpaired state. See, also, *conservation.*

Progress
A relative term, used here to indicate positive, qualitative and quantitative advancement. Progress occurs when a human social group moves toward improved social and environmental living standards. Progress embraces *development* but goes beyond to include measures of value more directly applicable in poorer communities, such as improvements in nutrition, shelter, health, communications and education.

Residuals
Materials or energy left over from a human economic activity and dumped upon the landscape, discharged into water bodies or diffused into the atmosphere. Residuals do not have a price on normal existing markets.

Soft (development, technology, energy, etc.)
An attitude toward the solution of a problem or the utilisation of a resource which upholds rusticity, labour intensiveness, the use of solar energy sources and environmental non-disruption. See, also, *balance.*

Synthetics
Substances which do not exist in nature. They are the product of human technical endeavour, designed or unintended, intentionally lethal or

benign, useful or *toxic*.

System

An assemblage of elements and institutions associated to form a complex unity; thus a mining system, an ecosystem, a development system.

Toxin (toxic)

An irritant or poison (organic, inorganic, or *synthetic*) which reacts detrimentally to the wellbeing of an *ecosystem* to which it is introduced.

1 Development in environmental perspective

In your World, there is a concern about
the quality of life; in our World, there is
concern about life itself.

Mahbub ul Haq, 1976[1]

The 'Third World',[2] Southern nations (see Diagram 1) or low income
countries, are a conglomerate of historical events, climatic variety, ethnic
alliances and resource admixture resulting in the condition most frequently described as underdevelopment; and at once it can be noted that,
relative to equilibrium, Southern underdevelopment is counterbalanced
by Northern overdevelopment. (The contrast is shown in Diagram 1.)

To describe a nation as materially underdeveloped is not in any way
to indicate that in qualitative or cultural terms it is at a lower level than
any other; indeed some countries with the most mature civilisations and
the most elaborate administrations are included in the materially underdeveloped category. The central issue taken up by this text is the binary
relationship which exists between mankind as consumer and environment
as provider, particularly as it affects Southern nations.

The development concept

The process, development, like the condition, underdeveloped, is an
expression with many meanings. Some employ the word when 'change'
alone is meant, others when they mean 'gain' or 'profit'. One helpful

1

Diagram 1 *The World: North and South,* illustrates the proportions of advanced and poor economies in a North and South context. This is done without reference to monetary measures, although a correlation is apparent. These representations show the area of each country in proportion to fossil fuel consumption (upper map) and in proportion to the number of inhabitants (lower map). *The upper and lower maps each cover the same area on the page.*

When a country is represented by approximately the same superficial area on the upper and lower maps (e.g. Mexico, Spain and Malaysia) then it is a matter of fine measurement to depict them as Northern or Southern, but in most other cases a country is either conspicuously greater in map area on the upper 'energy' diagram, and thus becomes labelled Northern, or conspicuously greater in map area on the lower 'population' diagram, thereby becoming labelled Southern. The maps deliberately avoid monetary depictions of gross and *per capita* national products and incomes because of the well recognised inaccuracies and contradictions inherent in monetary measures. Not, of course, that this apparently concrete depiction of human population patterns is infallible. The aggregates leave out, for example, the use of firewood and dried dung in energy consumption. What is shown here are relative proportions; but as a guide to scale, Mexico on the upper diagram represents about 70 million tons of coal equivalent, whereas on the lower diagram it represents about 70 million people.

Data reference: *United Nations Demographic Yearbook(s)* and Fremont Felix, *World Markets of Tomorrow,* (1972), London : Harper.

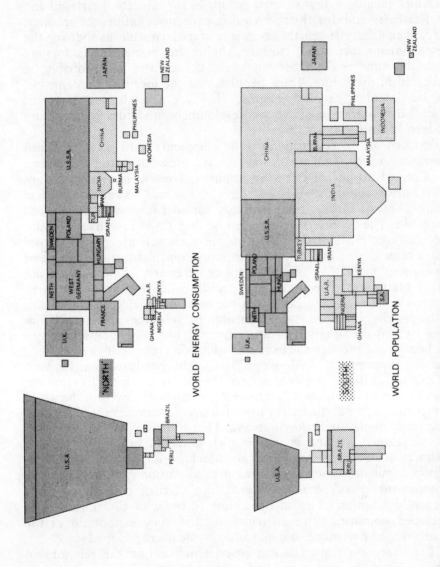

WORLD ENERGY CONSUMPTION

NORTH

WORLD POPULATION

SOUTH

DIAGRAM 1 THE WORLD : NORTH AND SOUTH

3

understanding of the term is that development implies change in favour of general human improvement, and change of two kinds, usually linked: expansion in consumption and enhancement of welfare. Development is thus both a material and an organisational matter.

Societies that do not seek improved change are few and far between. Examples include a few isolated groups in the Amazon heartland and the Kalahari: and for them, provided exogenous influences are kept away, their lifestyles remain essentially static. This means that for the present inhabitants, food, clothing, shelter and population factors are much the same as for those who went before, and will probably be replicated in the future. These peoples, and the localities they inhabit, can be described as *pre*developed. They are a small part of global society. By contrast, we have overdevelopment, underdevelopment and ecodevelopment.

Two primary forces fashion *over*development; mankind as technical innovator and mankind as cultural diffuser. Flows of matter and energy are directed to increase human comfort, convenience and pleasure whilst human conscience is largely directed towards domination.[3] These nations show no inclination to seriously consider any materially reduced alternative. They comprise free enterprise (e.g. USA) as well as centrally directed (e.g. USSR) nations. The people of these lands construct more shelter than can be lived in, produce more food than can be eaten and move about more than is meaningful or necessary. These qualities are not of themselves objectionable, especially when seen from within an overdeveloped economy. But when the locally available natural wealth of the Northern nations is supplemented by resources abstracted from other nations the situation becomes harmful; not only because of waste but because of the way the excess consumption rebounds as a denial of basic life support in underdeveloped lands. This condition is highlighted in Diagram 2. Illustrated here is, first, the extent to which the comfort, convenience and pleasure of overdeveloped minorities exceeds the world average and, second, the extent to which overdevelopment is dependent upon continuing underdevelopment. This leads to the depiction of *under*developed nations as those which have not been able, through historical accident (colonisation) or a lack of imperative (China), to fashion dominant monetary and resource allocation systems. Of course such nations always wanted to grow out of their poverty and they frequently attempt to do so by joining forces with the already over-developed countries. The difficulty is that they cannot do as the overdeveloped have done so much as do as the overdeveloped say.

There are two main characteristics which define the relationship between overdevelopment and underdevelopment:

1 Distribution of the goods of life is grotesquely out of balance. one distinguished authority claims that Americans get through biospheric resources at least 500 times faster than the people

of India; another, that the average developed world citizen consumes thirty times more than their counterparts in low income nations, and yet another that the current population growth of Northern nations places at least eight times as much pressure on natural resources as the population growth in Southern nations.[4] A degree of imbalance is always to be expected, particularly between nations, but gross privilege mirrored by gross deprivation of this order should be intolerable to any society.

2 For the larger low income countries internal imperialism is a matter for internal concern. Nobody assumes that Africans will not oppress Africans, or Asians other Asians—but Northern nation imperialism is altogether different. Even though the formal colonial era is substantially a feature of the past, the exogenous influence of the multinationals, the hegemony of the power blocs and the external funding and trading controls are still binding.

*Eco*development is altogether different. Here the concern is for self-reliance: neither to capture other countries' resources nor to give way to interlopers. Of course it is understood that no nation, however large, can stand alone. Thus ecodevelopment indicates a 'best fit' attempt to optimise the balance between population numbers, locally available resources and culturally desired lifestyles. Burma and Tanzania are markedly different from each other and from China, but ecodevelopment, or something close to it, characterises recent advances in all those countries. Such nations approach the ecodevelopment ideal. The pity is that, apart from some interest in environmental protection, the already overdeveloped nations have not been equally attracted.

A moral case, of deep concern, arises where it is proven that Northern prosperity is the result of Southern denial. But beyond this it is not so well appreciated that Northern prosperity, through the profit and consumption syndrome, creates a disordering of resources, both North and South. China demonstrates that the North—South shackle can be broken and replaced by moderate, locally appreciated, prosperity. There is no economic reason for the North to breach the shackle, whereas there is every reason, morally and materially, for the poorer nations to weigh the short term denials and long term advantages in pursuing self-reliance and self-sufficiency. Ecodevelopment can alleviate locally felt problems of inadequate clothing, shelter and nutrition. Environmental balance in any human ecosystem predicates a future for that society that can last as long as the present rate of solar energy support continues. A perpetration of current claims upon irreplacable resources by ever increasing human numbers suggests increased human misery and environmental degradation.

This diagram has to be viewed with caution because it depicts aggregate monetary values. A shift in the ascription of those monetary values (say upwards in the case of raw materials and downwards in the case of consumer durables) could, at a stroke, greatly alter the dispositions shown.

The imbalance inherent in the diagram suggests a need for consumer limitation in the North and birth limitation in the South, both policies moving towards an equalisation of population numbers and trade. In fact the current trend, which will probably continue until the year 2000, is for the Northern dominance of trade to be maintained and for Southern populations to expand, to about 85 per cent of the world total.

Trade between North and South has been shown split into its 14 per cent Northward and 15 per cent Southward bands because the 1 per cent difference has, over time, accumulated as the $300 billion (1979) debt of the Southern nations.

Data reference: restated from information on developed, centrally planned and developing countries supplied in the World Bank, *Annual Reports*, New York: UNCTAD, Part 1.

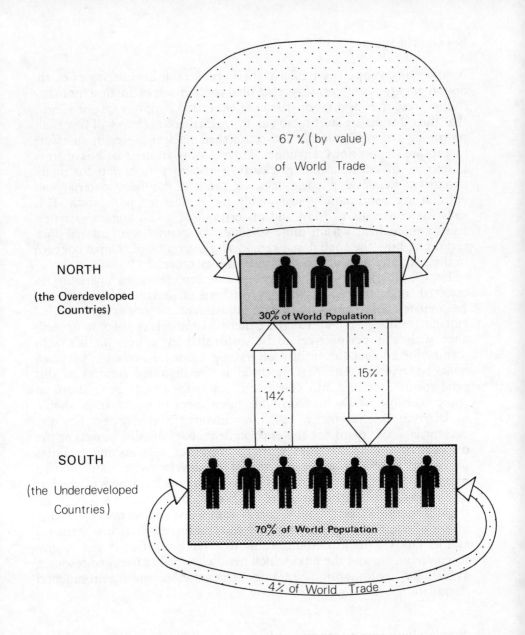

67 % (by value)
of World Trade

NORTH

(the Overdeveloped
Countries)

30% of World Population

14%

.15%

SOUTH

(the Underdeveloped
Countries)

70% of World Population

4% of World Trade

THE NORTH - SOUTH TRADING RELATIONSHIP
DIAGRAM 2

Beyond the present

A study of entropy (particularly the irrecoverable disordering of earth-bound energy resources) suggests global conflict and extinction for many if the present consumption patterns continue. Simply expressed, now that the oil wells are starting to run dry, Northern nations will flex their remaining economic muscle and rattle their nuclear sabres in an effort to capture the precious remainder. Moving away from situations of gross unfairness in consumption is clearly a necessary first step for many countries. Ecodevelopment seeks to provide the best material and cultural life continuously sustainable for the desired population. This calls for conscious concern and understanding by all human societies, and by individuals within those societies. Diagram 3 is a notional illustration of how the spatial and temporal dimensions of human concern in the past, and present, need to shift in the future.

For Southern nations ecodevelopment represents an upgrading in material consumption; by contrast Northern nations must anticipate and be prepared to accept a downward adjustment. Economic systems that expand resource take-up for the benefit of minorities have, in accordance with this perspective, to be surplanted by policies of life with dignity for all. Yet the futility of arguing a case for those not yet born must be avoided. The first essential is the dignified survival of this generation extending into continued fitness for human generations to come. Because of the unacceptable imbalances in world trade shown in Diagram 2, the change called for involves not only reversing the present lack of regard for the environment, but equating powers at the disposal of human societies with the resource replenishing facilities of nature. Empirically the pursuit of ecodevelopment rests on two premises: firstly, a recognition of the constraining influences of the law of entropy, most particularly the long term consequences arising from the disordering of earthbound energy resources; and secondly, a recognition of the consumptive power of cultural forces, particularly theism and its link via the protestant ethnic to capitalism, atheism and its link to communism, and the links which pantheism makes between resource availability, consumption, resource regeneration and environmental degradation.

Ecodevelopment: macro principles

The elements in the eleven point package which follows cannot be disassociated; ecodevelopment must be viewed integrally, although it may be pursued on a number of fronts, of which the first three are organisational.

Organisational point 1: establish an ideological commitment

Political cohesion is essential during the early years of ecodevelopment in order to generate the necessary political will to break with Northern insistence to compete on Northern terms and to avoid a replication of Northern mistakes. Confidence in the policy objective and a commitment to achieve this over a relatively long time scale are essentials.

Organisational point 2: sharpen political and administrative integrity

The correlation of official lassitude and public dishonesty with national malaise can hardly be overdrawn. If ecodevelopment, with an emphasis upon social equity, is to get under way, entrenched corruption and petty inefficiencies in bureaucracy must be scotched.

Organisational point 3: attain international parity

Because the control of capital carries more command than population numbers, the attainment of Southern nation parity is an issue which even the democratic faction in the Northern bloc finds itself loath to endorse. Cornering or even substantially participating in capital control is understandable as a desire but it represents futile tactics for low income nations. They are no real monetary threat to the economically developed nations even though their potential for military confrontation is emerging. More relevant for them is improving parity on international fora as a right they are prepared to assert. From a Northern nation perspective this may appear as advocacy for the end of worthwhile life as they have known it; but in fact, for them too, trade adjustments favourable to low income nations, and the self-reliance this will engender in the over-developed regions fire a guarantee for survival which current development models do not provide.

Material point 4: alleviate poverty-hunger

Hunger is the issue, poverty a main cause: hence poverty-hunger. The route to the alleviation of poverty-hunger in terms of ecodevelopment principles is clear: share out more fairly the unprocessed food resources that are already available and expand the band of those in employment by regulating job displacement through technological uptake, whilst also furthering the development of indigenous skills of agriculture, industry and construction.

Material point 5: eradicate disease-misery

Misery is the issue, disease the main cause: hence disease-misery. Preventative public health policies appeal to those Northern nations which

The upper graph in this diagram illustrates the narrow spectrum of concern in times past for the locally perceived world. A large proportion of people today live within this same perspective; but, as the middle graph depicts, a greater proportion of the global population now reach out beyond parochial and immediate interests. The lower graph depicts the notion of further spatial outgrowth and temporal extensions of concern.

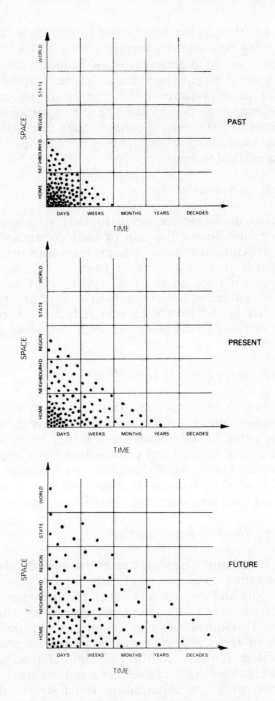

DIAGRAM 3 THE ALLOCATION OF HUMAN CONCERN

11

are giving out health aids; but being cured in this life is the preoccupation of those living now and this precept cannot be foregone in favour of future generations. Thus preventative public health measures have to run in tandem with curative medicine. Another important aspect is that the degree of self-reliance within the health services of poorer nations can be improved: first by banning the importation of most of the drugs offered at extortionate costs through international dealers; and second by establishing a hierarchy of decentralised health posts staffed by para-medical workers.

Material point 6: reduce arms

It is commonplace in low income nations for the foreign exchange investment in arms to be double the sum of hard currencies allocated to industrial and agricultural expansion. Gains from arms reduction can be double accounted; first as savings in foreign investment and non-productive labour, and second as a bonus injection of capital and skills for industry, agriculture and commerce. International parity (see point 3) is a policy matter bound closely to arms reduction. Agreeing to live peacefully (or agreeing to disagree) can result in massive accretions to ecodevelopment.

Material point 7: move closer to self-sufficiency

Although it is neither wholly necessary nor fully practical for any nation to be entirely self-reliant, it is clearly desirable to move in that direction. The two main stems to self-sufficiency are: (a) be as self-reliant as possible in the supply of food and construction materials; (b) establish socially acceptable low demand thresholds for consumer durables so that as much as possible is made at home, and only those functional essentials beyond local manufacturing capability are imported.

Material point 8: clean up urban squalor

Urban squalor is the most degrading human environmental condition. It is pathological rather than natural. Urban improvement involves the provision of supply and disposal services as curative measures, coupled to an identification of and adherence to parameters for urban function, form and size. This introduces the complex administrative task and moral problem of restricting the rights of people to move and settle where they will in response to the economic and human forces of attraction and repulsion. One answer is to fashion rural renewal as a counterattraction to urban opportunity. Rural structural reforms in terms of access to employment, education and medical services must counterweigh against urban profligacy. This requires the denial of any

12

rural tax support for urban lifestyles apart from the special requirements of national and regional government.[5]

Material point 9: balance human numbers with resources

Population limitation through birth control has little appeal in Southern nations where the large family is idolised and children are seen as a social investment. Yet in poor, densely settled lands, reduced numbers enables more to be shared. Achieving the threshold limits required to balance population with food production from renewable resources depends upon the use of socio-economic measures. This policy works well in soundly structured societies. In poorer countries direct material incentives may have to be introduced. One point is certain; social incentives serve more effectively to limit births than the advertisement of interruptive techniques.

Material point 10: conserve resources

The husbandry of renewable resources (soils, water, flora and fauna) is vital to life. The conservation of non-renewable resources (fossil fuels, minerals) is an altogether different matter which raises the question, for whom and why might they be conserved? The main case which any Southern nation, well off in terms of non-renewable resources, must weigh up is whether material enhancement for short term profits balances against resource scarcity in the future. Ecodevelopment does not stand in the way of non-renewable resource extraction, but it would direct: (a) that it be subject to full impact assessment; (b) that it be conducted piecemeal, winning every ounce possible; and (c) that locally available technology is used as fully as practicable.

Material point 11: protect the environment

The protection of urban heritage and the preservation of rural flora and fauna are, of course, desirable; but in terms of the poor masses, these are hardly imperatives. It is in urban areas that the need for environmental protection is more clearly apparent. Basic needs include running water in households, the disposal of household refuse and facilities to defecate with reasonable dignity.

Contemplation of the above eleven points is necessary as a preliminary to initiating political, administrative and operational action in the direction of ecodevelopment. The emanation from such action is of three parts. The social essence is that the value of dignified human existence arises from each and every individual's sense of wellbeing and usefulness; the resource conservation essence lies with the material benefits that can be gained from equitable resource utilisation now and for those yet to be born in the future: the environmental protection essence arises from creating a secure and attractive habitat. Ecodevelopment shows an alternative, shorn of political pre-alignment to capitalist or communist precepts, by which an alternative approach to material consumption can result in greater human progress.

The discussion so far suggests that there are aspects of human progress for low income regions which are not synonymous with economic growth; and that such economic growth and human progress which is possible within the context of ecodevelopment is a function of resources and population. Created wealth is seen here as fundamentally a product out of nature. The expansion of human numbers and of material consumption in the search, using classical development models, to create wealth, compounds poverty in limited resource regions. The reality is that tax and tariff manipulations, together with external capital borrowing, contributes only marginally, and unequally, to development. It is argued here that in the long term, human progress for low income regions can be achieved only through the adoption of an alternative policy attitude. This is where economic and environmental precepts, expressed jointly as ecodevelopment, can align resource conservation and protection of the habitat with the acceptable parts of earlier economic development models. This new form of policy is also able to include such basic human rights issues as roles for women, emancipation, youth and minorities which conventional policies cannot embrace. For the lower income Southern nations, average lifestyles cannot worsen. A socially, economically and environmentally balanced, and thus an improved future, offering progress for all, lies in the restructuring of internal order through joint (economic and environmental) ecodevelopment.

This introductory chapter includes what might seem at first sight to be an overreaction to low income circumstances, and includes some generalised reforms. Part I of the text which follows shows in more detail just how current development models are predicated to attain selective economic growth from the top down. Part II moves on to the offensive through the expression of an alternative, progressive policy, committed to the attainment of overall human progress worked from the bottom up. Part III outlines the principles involved in the fulfilment of the alternative ecodevelopment strategy.

14

Notes

1 Mahbub ul Haq, *The Poverty Curtain*, Columbia University Press, New York, 1976.

2 The expression 'Third World' was originally introduced to represent a bloc of 77 poorer nations frequently aligned in policy against the West (the Second World). The club of 77 has increased to over 100, and there is now frequent reference to the very poor component as the Fourth World—although this term is also used from time to time to describe the OPEC nations. Refer to work done by Fremont Felix, *World Markets of Tomorrow*, Harper and Row, London, 1972.

3 This trace, and one of the better general expositions on ecology, is outlined by I.G. Simmons, *The Ecology of Natural Resources*, Edward Arnold, London, 1974. A comparable North American text by P.R. Ehrlich, A.H. Ehrlich and J.P. Holdren is *Ecoscience*, Freeman, San Francisco, 1977.

4 The 500 factor is mentioned by Barbara Ward and Rene Dubos, *Only One Earth*, Pelican Books, London, 1972, p.176. The thirty times factor is mentioned by Godwin Matatu, *Development and the Human Environment.* The eight times factor appears in Mahbub ul Haq, *The Poverty Curtain*, Columbia University Press, New York, 1977, p.125.

5 For an authoritative review of urban bias in development, which includes a study of the conflict between rural and urban classes, refer to Michael Lipton, *Why Poor People Stay Poor*, Temple Smith, London, 1977.

PART I

INTRODUCTION

The two chapters which follow provide an interpretation of the character of underdevelopment in low income nations. Readers with an understanding of tropical ecosystems and resource platforms (Chapter 2) or with knowledge of human factor proportions in low income regions (Chapter 3) may prefer to pass lightly through this section to Part II.

2 Resources and ecosystems

You did not make the land. It is only yours to use for a short space of time but long enough to undo thousands of years of natural soil building processes. If you keep your soil in place and practise all we have learned about fertility improvement, you can then pass it on to its next custodian with the satisfaction of having exercised good stewardship and with the knowledge that it can be more productive of food than when you took it over.

K.C. Barrons, 1975[1]

There is historical evidence to establish that the abuse of landed resources, first soils and now fossil fuels, has borne a direct relationship to the coming to power of nation states. Diagram 4 shows how closely contemporary fossil fuel consumption equates with monetary wealth. The consequences of the resource degradation which results from this pattern of resource use are written on the landscapes of most nations. Max Nicholson and Erik Eckholm tot up the damage page by page in their writings; their awful testimony to the accelerating destruction of environmental resources in the face of ever larger populations is hindsight which has to be heeded.[2] Notwithstanding this, it does appear that the lower income countries do have less cause for alarm environmentally than those countries whose economic overdevelopment has led to resource depletion. So, do the Southern nations have a problem

This is a diagram about which little that is agreeable can be observed. In the bottom left hand corner are data for a group of countries which represent the poorer two billions of the world's people; and here fossil fuels are so relatively exhorbitant that animal dung, which should be returned to the soil, and trees which give shade and provide building materials are burned as domestic fuel. At the top right hand corner fossil fuel profligacy is represented by that sixth of the world's people using 60 per cent of the world's energy produced in this form. By the end of the century it will be unprofitable to burn oil and solar energy and coal will once again dominate the energy scene. Nuclear fuelled power systems still have technical problems and offer at best a partial solution in the short term for a few nations.

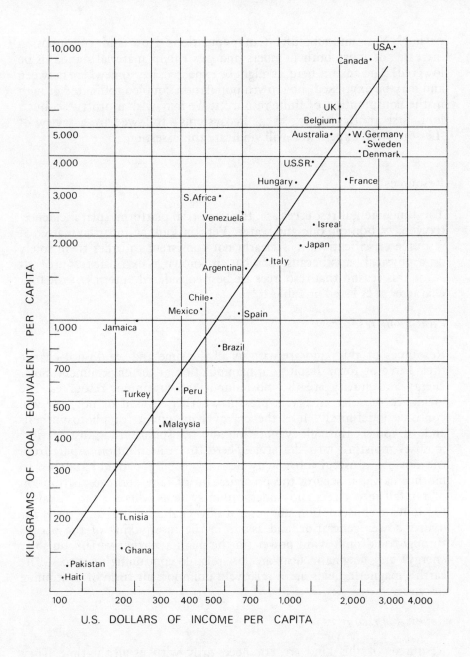

DIAGRAM 4   ENERGY AND INCOME

or not? Yes, undoubtedly. Can populations grow and consumption increase, or must both numbers and *per capita* material standards be lowered? The answer here, as might be expected, lies somewhere between and may be expressed: no-growth population coupled to limited growth in the consumption of finite resources. We may wish it otherwise, but a look first at 'Resources', then 'Ecosystems', followed by a review of 'Lessons from experience' will vindicate this assertion.

Resources

The fundamental resources are, the terrestrial platform, solar incidence, oxygen, carbon dioxide and water. Yet, on looking into the matter of resource classification, it is clearly not consistent to order them solely on a physical basis because of what are known as extrinsic resources. It is for this reason that resources are best considered in terms of the four characteristics listed in Table 1.[3]

Continuing resources

Resources of this kind are with us all the time and we do not change their force or form despite our manipulation of the environment. Solar energy and gravity are the most important continuing resources. The incidence of solar energy is present whether utilised or not, and will continue indefinitely. It is the energy component for photosynthesis and, of course, through evaporation and transpiration (against gravity) it raises moisture into the atmosphere for redistribution. Apart from the obviously useful job gravity does in keeping mankind attached to mother earth, it secures the precipitation of rain, and the distribution of rainfall into rivers and underground systems where it can be raised for human consumption and use; it also enables water to be used for hydro power generation and assists in the intermixing of the oceans through tidal pull. Wind power (in the main a further variant on solar energy) and magmatic heat are less reliable continuing resources. The earth's magnetic fields are a relatively unimportant form of continuing resource.

Renewable resources

Resources of this kind are not necessarily with us all the time. They include such 'free goods' as clean air, fresh water and the natural fauna and flora associated with all global life and could, therefore, also be described as the life sustaining resources. In an isolated and reasonably balanced ecosystem such as Antarctica, these renewable resources would go on, like continuing resources, for just as long as the sun shone. How-

Table 1

The four worldly resources

Class	Form	Character	Functional uses	Future
Continuing resources	Solar Gravitation Air and wave motion Magnetic	In regular 'continuing' supply	Energy input to life support	Continuing
Renewable resources	Clean air Clean water Natural flora Natural fauna Living soils	Flowing but of relative fixed supply varying in quality according to the purity of the ecosystem	Pollutant dispersal, environmental cleansing, life support	Impaired purity
Non-renewable* resources	Non-living minerals and fossil fuels	Fixed quantity	Energy synthesis, structures, protection and ornamentation	Depletion
Extrinsic resources	Human institutions and man made artefacts	Both incorporeal (institutions) and corporeal (artefacts)	In nature—none. Accessories to human existence	Some atrophication Some conservation

* Non-renewable resources do not exhibit significant rates of regeneration. They can be considered under two sub-headings, *Recycled non-renewable resources*, such as gold, copper, lead, that are largely retained for further use; and *Disposed non-renewable resources*, such as the cheaper metals, oil and coal, and mineral construction materials.

ever, the situation is rather less idyllic in the heavily populated countries and in wealthier nations where there is more cleaning and replenishing to be done than the ecosystem can handle. The net result is less clean water and air and a reduction in biotic diversity—in other terms, the global ecosystem has changed for the worse. As human populations grow and burn fossil fuels at rates which overload the cleaning power of the biosphere, and manufacture persistent and harmful toxins which are foreign to and poisonous in nature, so they reduce the amount, diversity and purity of renewable resources.

Non-renewable resources

Resources of this kind are inorganic and for all practical purposes they are not added to by nature, nor can they be manufactured by mankind. They are the minerals of the earth and the fossil fuels laid down in the past. They are sometimes described as being in fixed supply. Material matter is indestructible, yet when raised by human agents these non-renewable resources are mostly transformed into discarded wastes. Only limited quantities of the more valuable metals are recycled for re-use. This characteristic of the way non-renewable resources are used requires that they be considered under two headings:

1 *Recycled non-renewable resources,* such as gold, copper and lead which have a scrap value that ensures their partial re-use. Other metals are almost worth recycling, especially aluminium; but until scrap prices rise as a result of increases in the cost of energy inputs for base metal refining (thereby making it attractive to collect and re-use these metals) they will continue to be discarded on tip heaps, probably for recycling at a later date. Recycling, in the case of aluminium, will increase because of the energy costs involved in mineral refining. It is quite apparent that metal made objects are used far longer in low income nations than elsewhere and that more care is already taken in these countries to recycle a higher proportion of the non-renewable resources embodied in capital goods.

2 *Disposed non-renewable resources* include such various materials as the iron and steel left in abandoned capital goods, the silver put into photographic salts and the mercury used in fungicides and herbicides. Depletions are not always serious, because of high reserves, and in any case substitutes can often be devised for the processes and manufactures which use many of these minerals. The depletion of fossil fuels is, however, a serious matter. Equally grave is the final deposit of gaseous, liquid and solid wastes, often as toxins and non-degradable substances in soils, waters and the atmosphere. The disposed

24

non-renewable resources are victims of the second law of thermodynamics (the entropic law) which establishes that as minerals (particularly fossil fuels) are used by mankind they are transformed from a useful form into disordered less useful forms. Thus burnt fossil fuel does not disappear from the face of the earth; but the heat, light, noise and particulate residuals resulting from combustion render it too randomly disordered for further re-use.

Extrinsic resources

Resources of this kind are either fabrications of the human hand, or are in the conscience of society. The tangible, extrinsic resources include the products of human skills in adapting landscapes for human habitation. Subjectively they are often considered ugly, as is the case with most of the early industrial regions, but nevertheless they have a monetary value. Occasionally they are considered aesthetically, as with a rural vista or a well designed urban space. It is a characteristic of the corporeal extrinsic resources that mankind can put a value on them, certainly a replacement value. With incorporeal extrinsic resources we also have to consider a cerebral investment that can vary from religious belief to capitalist fervour. Indeed the character of one may explain the other. A Papuan, claiming that the land owns him rather than that he owns the land, regards land in itself as a form of institutional security: and do not Western millionaires accumulate unspent money as their form of institutional security? Incorporeal extrinsic resources largely represent what human beings, in one important sense, live and strive for.

Resource exploitation

The most rapacious usage arises in connection with the exploitation of fossil fuels, ocean fish stocks, tropical hardwoods, agricultural soils and mineral deposits. Of these, fossil fuels are dominant because it is from this form of energy that other resources, or substitutes for them, are produced. Royalties may be paid with a view to conserving stocks and some payment may be settled on people who hold a proprietary interest; but generally the main operational criterion is exploitation without a regard or responsibility for the consequences.[4] A closer look at the economics of fish exploitation will explain this more clearly.[5]

In the late 1950s and early 1960s Peru caught more fish than any other nation, and did so off its own coastline. Indeed, Peru caught enough fish (12.3 million tons in 1970) to furnish an adequate protein contribution to the diet of everybody in India. But the Peruvian catch went to Europe and North America as cheap animal and poultry feed.

It was a sad example of a poor country selling a valuable resource cheaply to wealthier nations. The immorality embedded in this transaction is bad enough when viewed in relation to starving Asia. Even worse, in ecological terms, is the fact that at 12.3 million tons the Peruvian catch was rapacious—too massive and too prolonged—and drastically affected the regenerative potential of the anchovy. As an example of resource exploitation this is on a parallel with the depletion of whale stocks. What has happened in both these industries is that those people who are in business to make a profit from such 'roaming', if not quite 'free' goods make greater, then even greater, investments of capital, and hence greater and even greater catches, in order to create the higher profit which the higher capital outlay anticipates. In this way, and because of the pressure of competitors also out to grab as much as possible as quickly as possible, this kind of resource exploitation eventually leaves everybody empty handed.

Consider also the exploitation of the phosphate caps on a few isolated islands in the Pacific. The Nauruans may have more trinkets than the Ocean Islanders; but both societies are left with moonscapes. This is an extreme example of almost complete environmental degradation due to mineral extraction, but the principles apply on a smaller scale to all other kinds of resource extraction. The heavy costs of exploration and production can only be met by producing ever increasing volumes of oil at the surface. Increases in the paper money price are ineffective simply because oil is such an important commodity that it is in effect a currency in itself, an energy currency, and should in fact be the basis for calculating real value.

Soil exhaustion

Resource exploitation, generally, is very much a phenomenon of this century. It is assisted by technological innovations and fossil fuelled power applied, as it were, as a consequence of human ambition. Soil resource exhaustion, however, is an area of exploitation with deep historical roots. Deserts are the measurable extreme condition arising from soil exhaustion. Of course, there are natural as well as man made deserts. Studies undertaken by the United Nations Environmental Programme show that 10 per cent of the world's landed surface is natural extreme desert, and that about 30 per cent of the earth's landed surface is semi-arid;[6] about one-fifth of these latter desert areas can be accounted for as recently human induced. There is nothing ecologically unsound about a natural desert. What is unsound is the induction of desertification (or desert creep) through soil degradation. This arises as a consequence of arbitrary divisions of semi-arid lands, colonial pacification, export-led development and access to fossil water resources; all of which could lead to unparallelled future desertification.

The facts of soil degradation are not always easy to get into focus. Mankind intervenes in the natural ecology of most of the globe's biosphere. People fashion their habitats. In the temperate zones human presence at high densities appears to be adaptive and longlasting. In the tropical zones people have settled at high densities on rain forest flood plains over centuries, until population increase is arrested by disaster, pestilence or war; but in the semi-arid tropics and the tropical uplands the fragility of soils has never allowed the human population to expand beyond what are often regarded as puzzlingly low densities. Soil fatigue explains the semi-arid scene; whereas soil erosion is important in the tropical uplands.

A semi-arid zone under attack from soil fatigue has arisen in dramatic contemporary terms in the Sahel of North Africa. The condition is also well known in the Middle East, on the Indian sub-continent, in Western Latin America and throughout central Australia. It is drought assisted, but the progenitor of damage is mankind and the beasts kept for security or veneration. One way of explaining this matter of land population balance is to compare semi-arid central India and semi-arid central Australia, both areas receiving an average of 250–270 mm of rain each year. In Australia only a quarter or half a sheep is sustained by each hectare. Profits are made at the rate of about one to three cents per hectare, yet in the aggregate they multiply to represent about half this wealthy nation's earnings from primary production. If there is prolonged drought in central Australia there is 'sheep misery'—a decimation of flocks.

In India, by contrast, four to eight people try to live on a hectare of semi-arid land. There are no profits of any kind and a prolonged drought leads directly to human decimation. This throws insight into land policy in semi-arid areas, namely that in the absence of irrigation they can only sustain low densities (half to one standard stock unit per hectare). Failure to observe this threshold causes nature to apply its own regulator, decimation by drought. Perfectly dry conditions may induce little more than wind erosion, which on balance is no great global offence to nature, for by driving off the human and animal predators these areas are put into store for a revival of vegetation with the later replenishment of water. It is arguable that droughts are largely induced by human beings and that one drought somehow induces another. Nature is indifferent. People in these areas must occupy land at low dispersed densities and conserve the water and floral basis of their life support. Societies are learning conservation, but they have yet to sufficiently respect the thresholds of human and animal carrying capacity. Although the central problem here is societal, the consequences for good or ill are starkly physical.

The tropical uplands under attack from soil erosion are among the most complex and delicate environmental systems on earth. The highlands of East Africa and the Cameroons, those of Java, New Guinea and Central Asia, together with the Andean highlands are represented here. They have often been viewed as stable 'like' the temperate zones, but the diurnal and annual variation in climate and extent of solar incidence is of course vastly different. Once the land has been cleared, heavy rains falling onto soils bound together by a weak organic structure induce sheet and gully erosion. Again the problem is one of carrying capacity; but, unlike the semi-arid zones, an even dispersal of population is not the answer. Unless used for tree crops, tropical upland must be worked both intermittently to allow the soils to regenerate, and selectively by keeping off steep slopes and by leaving large tracts of forest, with as many as twenty units of land out of production for each one being cultivated. Except that the pattern of soil erosion is different, the problems of the large wet tropical river basins such as the Amazon and the Congo are much the same. Biomass of impressive quantity and apparent diversity exists in the tropics, but it is invariably of relatively useless quality and these environments reject the introduction of alien flora and fauna.

Resource exhaustion, and particularly soil degradation, has been shown to arise as a consequence of increasing man-to-land ratios. Environmental factors are fundamental inputs to the equation: a human being may need ten hectares of semi-desert in the Sahel and only a tenth of a hectare in the Red River delta. Social and technological criteria also modify the situation; a Javanese highlander manages agriculture more effectively than his Cameroon counterpart, although their environments are superficially fairly similar. Where the threshold lies, and what constitutes equilibrium, are matters that can only be established empirically.

Water resource depletion

Fossil water deposits might be replenished slowly after abstraction—or they might not. In the latter case the raising and use of such supplies in order to save drought stricken Rajasthan, for example, or to desalinate the Indus Plain, might compound the ultimate problem of survival. No case for wholly ignoring the use of fossil water resources is advanced; it is simply contended that fossil sources should only be used sparingly and in times of emergency, unless it can be established that annual restocking will take place. Reliance on fossil water resources by human multitudes in the northern parts of the Indian sub-continent is a disturbing recent phenomenon.

Nearer the surface, but still within the ground water category, are those natural, replenishable water supplies in acquifers and water lenses. These are usually saline to some extent. The supplies here are replenished, and it is the rate of replenishment that regulates the rate of abstraction.

This point can best be made at a small scale with reference to the 'fresh' water lens of island atolls. Here rainwater percolates down through the sand and adds to the lens of fresh to brackish water which is contained by the surrounding ocean. The lens moves up and down with the tidal flux. In order to obtain potable water, trenches are dug longitudinally along the centre of the atoll down to a level where a brackish pool is formed at high tide. This water can be abstracted at empirically determined rates depending on rainfall and the time elapsed since the last rain. When the brackish water is abstracted too rapidly the ocean percolates in, and such salt water requires fifteen years of rains before it is flushed out. The historical price for excessive water abstraction on an isolated atoll was death.

Surface irrigation systems, of which the Indus Plain, the Punjab and the China Plains are examples, lead to salinity. In this way 'Pakistan was losing a hectare of good agricultural land (in the 1960s) every twenty minutes, but gaining a new claimant on that land by birth every twenty-four seconds'.[7] Here the problem was one of excessive irrigation which raised the water table to the surface, causing waterlogging and the bringing up of salts in solution.

The big hydro schemes of Africa have also led to environmental and economic shortcomings which tend to outweigh their material advantages. Lake Aswan may indeed be full of silt before it is ever full of water; it has never produced the power it was designed to generate and an unwelcome side effect has been a dwindling of the delta fish catch. The Volta, in flooding some of the best bottom land in Ghana and cutting all north—south communication in the country, has obviously cost more than it has produced for the internal economy. Economically the Kariba project did more for local people because it literally brought light and power into so many homes, but the environmental problems of surface weeding and extension of *bilharzia* were unforseen. In all these cases the stricture is not to inhibit dam building but to see, as with the Mahaweli scheme in Sri Lanka, the Damodar project in India and the Bicol River project in the Philippines, that a better approach is co-ordinated river basin and national development rather than power exploitation at the dam face.

A somewhat controversial point can be made in relation to urban water supply. The fact here is that on the one hand access to potable water is denied to two-thirds of the world's people and they are thus visited by sicknesses directly related to this denial, yet the other third of the world's population receives supplies at excessively high standards of both purity and quantity. The generalisation might be disproved in specific cases, but the contention is that often the standards of purity and quantity of supply in large urban areas exceed those needed. Mixed supply systems with cart delivered potable water and a piped general supply is one alternative to consider.

The most appropriate way to view the energy cycle is to form separate understandings of the fossil fuel 'stored energy' source and the 'living energy' force provided by the sun. The day by day utilisation of this 'living energy' force is explained later in this chapter with illustrations of the biospheric cycle and the oxygen–CO_2 cycle.[8] The complete energy cycle ultimately involves the laying down of such dead organic matter as coal, oil and gas. Indeed the final stage in this cycle underpins twentieth century technological advance. Yet the vast difference between the rate of contemporary consumption of fossil fuels and the rate at which decomposers are laid down renders the complete energy cycle an academic curiosity. It is for this reason that in Table 1 the fossil fuels fit into the non-renewable resource section. Concerned societies would conserve these resources through measured abstraction. This is the middle road between profligacy and preservation. But there are errors of overstatement as well as understatement for, of the fossil fuels under dry land, oil, the convenience fuel, forms only a small part: coal still exists in relative abundance. Furthermore, the water covered surface of the globe is about double the landed area. Fossil fuels that have gravitated to deposits under the sea bed could prove greater than those now nearly exhausted under dry land. The law governing the rights of exploitation, and penalties for pollution outside international zones are vital matters for the immediate future because the technology for sea bed exploitation is rapidly being perfected.

The hastening metabolism of fossil fuels may, on the one hand, establish mildly different 'adaptive' global ecosystems; but on the other it may lead to permanent and undesirable environmental changes. The facts of the matter are neither easily garnered nor interpreted. We know that mankind is consuming fossil fuels at a rate which would have been considered unbelievable at the dawn which heralded the era of the combustion engine, and that about half of this particular form of metabolism takes place in North America. We also know that during the last 25 years there has been an increase of about 3 per cent in the measurable amount of carbon dioxide in the atmosphere. Is this all, and is much of this extra carbon dioxide being laid down through photosynthesis as extra biomass? We cannot be sure. Another factor is that climatic shifts which mankind collectively might rather do without, such as longer dry spells in some areas and previously unheard of deluges in others, might be another causal consequence. A further question arises; does the extra carbon dioxide now in the global ecosystem retain heat that would otherwise reflect to space? Or might it be cutting down the amount of solar heat we receive? Again, we cannot yet be sure. The world does seem to be locked into a new pattern of climate. There will indeed be ill winds even if there are some benefits; a watered desert here, warmer temperate zone there; but because human settlement has grown to adapt to one spatial order of biomass distribution, human suffering will inevitably result however the climatic order is altered.

The human consequences arising from the fact that fossil fuels are essentially non-renewable are diverse and will intensify in complexity as time goes by. The view put forward here is that the modern history of the world is very much reflected in the way the 'holders', the Northern nations, convert fossil fuels for their own ends at ever increasing rates. This will tail off. There may be some nasty squabbles over the final scraps, and it is hoped that nuclear force will not be used, but in general there seems to be no need to lament this scenario either materialistically or ecologically. Fossil fuels were laid down from the biotic resources of the past; they are now being put back into circulation. It is one thing to moralise about the profligacy of this metabolism, and quite another to indicate new energy policies.

One effect which has already been observed in low income areas is that the lessening use of fossil fuel based fertilisers results in lowered crop yields and soil exhaustion. Fossil fuels do not contribute much in the way of biotic nutrients to plants, but are mainly used to manufacture essential minerals of which only nitrogen can be readily supplied by N-fixing legumes. Less demanding crops, such as cassava, will have to be considered more seriously for food and alcohol fuel fermentation from sugar production in the future. Another effect of fossil fuel shortage has been that of price increases for white spirit, paraffin and bottled gas. Formerly available at give away prices, their scarcity has led to a stripping of forest cover and the burning of dung patties for domestic fuel.

But, on the whole, fuel for mankind in low income countries will always be available in ways that are hardly mysterious. First there is the eternal sun and its direct warmth. Second, there is the very efficient solar based creation of carbohydrate energy through photosynthesis. Future tropical living people will be comfortable, and can always have the use of fuel adequate to their needs. As yet the plant breeding of fuel crops that are photosynthetically effective has received scant attention given the efficient combusion of such fuels to produce convertible energy. The future life support of tropical people in the poorer countries is not something to become unduly alarmed about; indeed, tropical people, unlike their temperate zone relatives, can look forward to comparative energy security. In poorer areas it may be that a more serious human problem will arise in the misuse of fossil water resources.

Ecosystems

There are many ways of ordering our thoughts about ecosystems; a biologist might rank them according to the stability of species at risk,

About 30 per cent of the solar energy received by the globe is immediately re-radiated. Some 47 per cent is absorbed into the earth's atmosphere, waters and land, and the remaining 23 per cent is used to power the hydrological cycle.

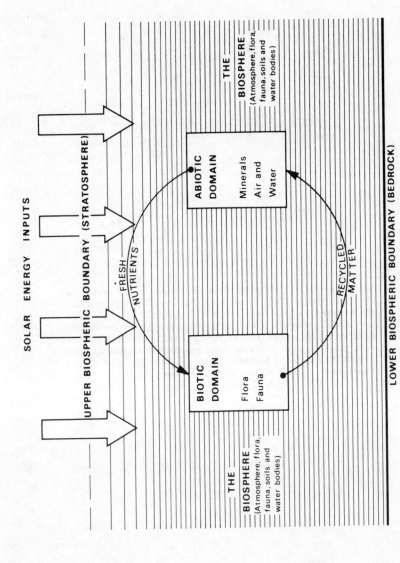

SOLAR ENERGY INPUTS

UPPER BIOSPHERIC BOUNDARY (STRATOSPHERE)

THE BIOSPHERE (Atmosphere, flora, fauna, soils and water bodies)

ABIOTIC DOMAIN

Minerals
Air and
Water

BIOTIC DOMAIN

Flora
Fauna

FRESH NUTRIENTS

RECYCLED MATTER

THE BIOSPHERE (Atmosphere, flora, fauna, soils and water bodies)

LOWER BIOSPHERIC BOUNDARY (BEDROCK)

THE BIOSPHERIC CYCLE

DIAGRAM 5

33

Land, water and air are all platform components in this cycle. The vast 'machine' is driven by the sun. This simplified diagram shows the oxygen–CO_2 cycle for plants only. Raising the CO_2 concentration in the biosphere as a whole may induce atmospheric overheating or other complications. Indeed, raising the CO_2 level in temperate zone glasshouses is a well established procedure for increasing plant growth. But as far as humans are concerned the supply of oxygen for oxidative metabolism is of prime importance.

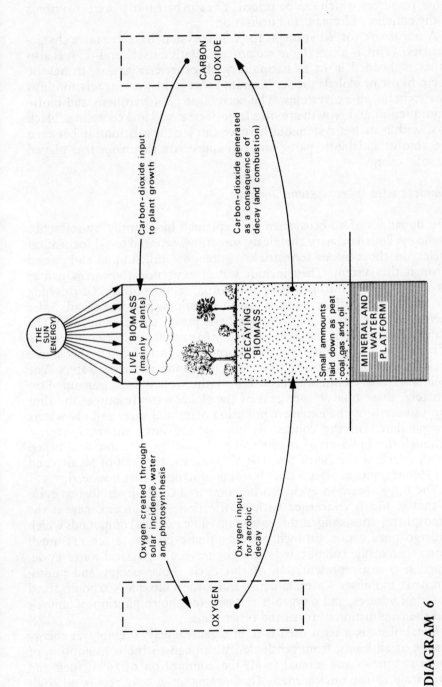

DIAGRAM 6

THE OXYGEN CARBON-DIOXIDE CYCLE

THE SUN (ENERGY)

LIVE BIOMASS (mainly plants)

DECAYING BIOMASS

Small ammounts laid down as peat coal, gas and oil

MINERAL AND WATER PLATFORM

Carbon-dioxide input to plant growth

Carbon-dioxide generated as a consequence of decay (and combustion)

CARBON DIOXIDE

Oxygen created through solar incidence, water and photosynthesis

Oxygen input for aerobic decay

OXYGEN

whereas an economist would rank them according to their demand on those resources which can be priced. The aim here is to place ecosystems in the context of human land utilisation.

A normative (or 'what ought to be') ecosystem has three main characteristics: (a) it is alive; (b) it reciprocates within itself; and (c) it is also either embedded in or in harmony with other ecosystems. It may be micro-biotic or global in scale. Diagram 5 shows the working relationships that exist in all ecosystems. The secrets of photosynthesis and biotic reproduction and growth are, to a large degree, still locked up in a 'black box' within such a system but here we can see the relationship between the abiotic and biotic parts, and can appreciate the major role played by solar energy.

Characteristic 1: ecosystems are alive

The dynamics of an ecosystem are explained biologically by reference to the cycling of primary chemicals, sometimes referred to as biochemical cycles. In these cycles terrestrial resources are called upon and passed through the system. They include water, oxygen, carbon (regarded as the key element), nitrogen and phosphorus, among others. Of this long list the oxygen-carbon cycle is worth examining in some detail. Solar energy and the 'magic' of photosynthesis power this organic life.[9] The hydrological cycle is the easiest to relate to everyday experience because of its physical tangibility. The main complexity introduced to this simple cycle is that of pollution, principally in ground and river waters. The pollutants are eventually flushed into the oceans for clean up. Fortunately, these hold 95 per cent of the global water resources and thus one can see how the extensive pollution of ground, river and like waters is assimilated in the course of time by the interconnected oceans, although the build up of toxins and pollutants in the more landlocked oceans, such as the Black Sea, the Yellow Sea, the Gulf of Mexico and the Mediterranean, offer a clear warning of dangers that lie ahead.

The oxygen-carbon cycle can be compared to the hydrological cycle in that it too is concerned with purification. The 'ocean' here is the atmosphere, consisting in this case of invisible gaseous compounds which undergo purification through photosynthetic change, a process much more chemically complicated than the generally physical water cycle. Diagram 6 is a representation of this cycle. Solar energy and photosynthesis mobilises water, minerals and carbon dioxide. Carbon is fixed as carbohydrates, and oxygen is released for the respiration of animals and the combustion of fossil and other fuels.

Metabolism is a term used here in a general way. It embraces energy change of all kinds, from gentle decay through to the consumption of crops as human and animal food, the combustion of fossil fuels and ultimately to the nuclear blast. The burning up of resources of all kinds

36

is bound to the law of metabolism: that for all practical purposes matter is indestructible and stays with us in one form or another.

The energy source which underwrites all ecosystems is the sun. The combustion of all the fossil fuel on the planet would be, set against the sun, to compare a candle to a hydrogen bomb. All the oil burned so far in all the cars ever made would not be enough to do the job the sun does in one month to vaporise water, carry it in clouds, then release it over the earth's surface—and this is just the solar input to the hydrological cycle. The solar engine is the power source we know and can trust; by contrast, nuclear fission on earth is a form of energy production involving colossal chemical and physical forces. Here mankind should proceed extremely cautiously.

Characteristic 2: ecosystems reciprocate within themselves

The interest which mankind ought to take in ecological cycles arises from the fact that human beings cannot live on sun and air alone. We are omnivorous and incapable of photosynthesis; although we dominate we are dependent on plants and animals for all our food supply. From a human perspective there are two main categories of life in the global biomass. First, there are the producers, usually plants, which are essentially self-nourishing and are able to sustain their species by applying solar energy and photosynthesis to inorganic inputs. They are the staff of life for the consumers which feed off plants, either directly as primary consumers or indirectly as secondary consumers (i.e. those who feed off the primary consumers). Human beings can be regarded as comprising a bit of both—they are omnivorous (primary and secondary) consumers.[10] Food chains, linkages and webs have always been the object of human curiosity.[11] Buddhism enshrines this recognition in behavioural laws; other non-Christian religions, often denigrated for their pantheism, go further to identify 'balance' within nature. Christian, capitalist and Marxian precepts have, on the whole, stressed the dominance of mankind over nature.

An important feature of food chains is that the biomass at each trophic (nutritional take up) level is only a fraction of that on which it feeds. Diagram 7 illustrates the nature of this relationship. It shows that at any point in time, for every kilogramme of predator there must be 200 kilogrammes of support biomass.[12] The human animal is not shown in this diagram. Their position is such that they tend, if unchecked, to eliminate the carnivorous competitors and feed omnivorously on flesh and vegetation. By shortening the trophic chain so that human beings consume more herbage, becoming say nine parts herbivore and only one part carnivore, it becomes possible for converted free ranges to support four times as many people. The lessons overall are that there are absolute limits to the number of people who can live off a vegetal biomass, and

This diagram is simplistic. Two of the more important complexities not considered in it are: (a) that the proportions can vary widely from those shown; and (b) that *homo sapiens* are part of the food chain. At low, pre-colonial, densities the human population competed with the lions as predators upon the herbivores. As human densities increased these carnivores were eliminated and are now mainly confined to game reserves; the human population then had the herbivores for themselves. But as human numbers (and thus the numbers of their cattle) increased, mankind was lowered a trophic peg to compete with herbivores for the use of the grassland. A future as agriculturalists offers a little food supply leeway in Central Africa, and a hope for the Sahel, but only if human numbers are kept in check.

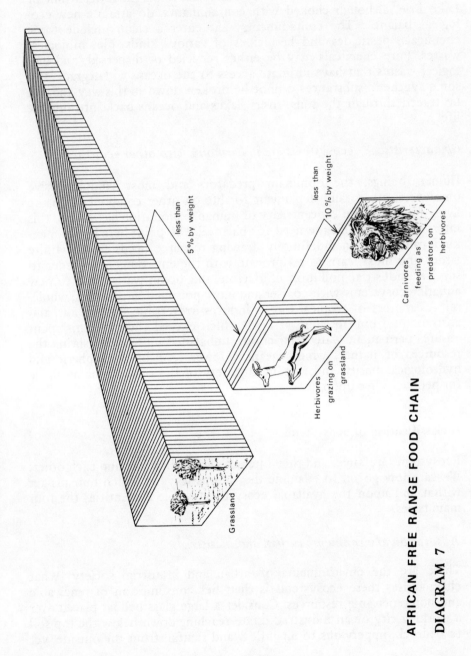

Grassland

less than
5% by weight

Herbivores
grazing on
grassland

less than
10% by weight

Carnivores
feeding as
predators on
herbivores

AFRICAN FREE RANGE FOOD CHAIN

DIAGRAM 7

that when human nutrition is threatened a reduction in the consumption of animal foodstuffs sustains a much larger human population.

Not all chains and webs are nutritional. There is the adverse flow of contaminants to consider. In strict ecological terms the lower Rhine or Lake Erie, although choked with contaminants, do attain a new ecological balance. The contaminants that enter a chain include toxic chemicals, pesticides and herbicides of various kinds, plus biological wastes. Pure chemicals may be either recycled or dispersed, and biological wastes that have ultimate access to the oceans will degrade, but some synthetic substances cannot be broken down in this way and can be traced through the soils, rivers, lakes and oceans back into organic life.

Characteristic 3: ecosystems are in harmony with other ecosystems

Human beings, the dominant predators and most comprehensive omnivores, are totally dependent for life on other components in the living biomass. The egocentricity of human exploitation has ignored this interdependency and the need for balance. The point here is that mankind cannot go on indefinitely drawing resource needs from a finite larder and must learn to reciprocate with the environment in order to survive. Industrial pollution of riverine and ocean waters lead to new aquatic ecosystems with coarser and more poisoned inhabitants; wholesale clearances of tropical forests induces irreversible soil erosion; and abstraction from aquafers at rates which exceed their replenishment ensures permanent water restrictions. Imbalance will serve to shrink the resources of nature, which means a lower level of atmospheric and hydrological purity and a reduced variety of flora and fauna available for people to live upon.

A classification of ecosystems

Ecosystems are alive, and they interact with themselves and each other. We can now go on to examine the various ways in which humans act within and upon the available ecosystems. Table 2 identifies the four main types.

Absorption environments (urban and industrial)

These are the environments of urban and industrial society. What characterises these ecosystems is their net consumption of renewable and non-renewable resources. Consider a large glass bell jar placed over a working city or an industrial estate reaching down below the top soil to bedrock, impervious to air inflow and rainfall from the outside, yet

Table 2
The four environments of mankind

Regime	Form	Function	Agent	Resource input	Processes	Products
Absorption environments	Urban synthesised	Human habitat	Mankind	Fossil fuels Imported food Minerals Bio-resources	Consumption Growth Survival	Institutions Residuals Services
Production environments	Rural synthesised	Food and fabric production	Mankind and Nature	Fossil fuels Fertilisers Pathogens Solar energy	Production through exploitation	Food Raw materials Waste
Composite ecosystems	Rural naturalised	Continual sustention of human life	Mankind and nature	Solar energy Rainfall Some fuels Fertilisers	Balanced production	Food Raw materials
Natural ecosystems	Natural	Equilibrium	Nature	Solar energy Rainfall	Eco-balance	Natural biomass

receiving sun and light through the glass and its regular supplies of raw materials through an airlocked hatch. Within a short time the inhabitants would be dead, choked in their own combustion as a prelude to being starved, drowned in sewerage or crushed by solid wastes. The example is imaginary, but there is a real illustration of the principle in the fantastic technology required to keep two or three people alive in a particular kind of closed off bell jar, the spaceship. The essential point here is that as resources are for all practical purposes indestructible, these absorption ecosystems produce solid, gaseous and liquid by-products whose bulk has to be dumped as waste back into the space beyond the city place or the factory. The oceans are treated as sinks, the countryside the repository for many non-biodegradable solids, and the four winds as the means for dispersing gases and airborne particulates.

Production environments

These are concerned with the macro-organisation and co-ordination of production for selected, economically desirable food and fabric goods. These essentially industrial—agricultural ecosystems (agribusinesses) are characterised by the singularity of agricultural production (monoculture) and the low diversity of associated natural flora and fauna. This makes them ecologically vulnerable. They use solar energy, but they are also major consumers of fossil fuel energy resources in that much more fossil fuel energy is put into agribusiness as chemical fertiliser than is gained in nutritional calories. Agribusiness also produces effluents and toxins for recycling elsewhere in the biosphere in accordance with the 'cowboy' economics of limitless exploitation of common property assets.

Composite ecosystems (agricultural settlement)

These are the ordered environments of self-reliant human settlement. They are characterised by stability, which is reflected in a reciprocal compatibility of inputs and outputs, considerable diversity of agricultural production and a low level of terminal waste.

Natural ecosystems (pre-developed land utilisation)

These are the nature dominated environments of the jungles, deserts, mountains and polar regions which are only sparsely used by mankind. If we were to place a bell jar over such an ecosystem, an isolated atoll for example, then life within could be sustained for a considerable time. Oxygen would be produced by plants for absorption by mammal, fish and fowl and because of the balance (without the creation of non-degradable toxins or a reliance upon external resources) the ecosystem would survive. Natural ecosystems are the 'sinks' for cleaning and re-cycling the wastes from absorption and production ecosystems.

What can be concluded from this designation of the four most readily identifiable ecosystems is that they are sub-parts of the global ecosystem. Convenient though the four way division may be, the dependence of the first two ecosystems (urban and production) upon the second (composite and natural) is a reality which human societies have to accept as cardinal.

Environmental effects of waste disposal

Cottrell gives a clear definition of the cost effects arising from the disposal of residuals:

> *Damage costs* are the direct costs of the pollution itself, e.g. the cost of bronchitis, in people afflicted by smog, or the cost of fish losses due to poisonous effluent discharged into a river. *Avoidance costs* are those incurred by people in attempting to separate themselves from pollution, e.g. the cost of sound-proofing a home to keep out the noise of aircraft or traffic. Both damage and avoidance costs are external costs and they can be large. *Transaction costs* are the costs of gathering information about pollution, especially by monitoring, and of preparing and administering anti-pollution policies. *Abatement costs,* which usually dominate discussions of pollution economics are those incurred in preventing or abating pollution, e.g. the cost of a sewerage treatment plant. There is a roughly inverse relation between damage and avoidance costs, on the one hand and transaction and abatement costs on the other. Where the latter are not large, the former will run high, and vice versa. Somewhere between lies the optimum.[13]

A nuisance can be described as a substance or an activity, whether bio-logically toxic or not, which is undesirable in a specific location over a period of time. Undesirability may vary from repugnance over the odour emanating from a sewage farm, through to the mild annoyance a golfer might express as a jet plane screams overhead while he tries to sink a putt. Pollution is a more serious matter. A pollutant causes an unacceptable material change in the environment or part of the environment.

Nuisances can be short term, of limited effect, and may disappear; pollutants endure and change the environment. In this way a dead whale on a beach is a *nuisance* generating biotic decay, whilst DDT is a toxic *pollutant.* Toxic pollution is caused by poisonous or irritable substances not generally known in nature and which materially change natural eco-systems by reducing biotic diversity and killing off some plant and animal species. They are not readily biodegraded and many of them persist in their toxicity over long periods of time or combine with other toxins or minerals to form synthetic compounds which are even more dangerous. Pollutants include such aesthetic irritants as plastic solids in the oceans, pathogens such as DDT in the soils, and synthesised gases and radio-activity in the atmosphere. They are almost entirely products of human technical endeavour.

With residuals one has really to be concerned with both cause and effect. There is a constant danger of cover up, the most serious being an application of the maxim 'the solution to pollution is dilution'. Clearly the total environment must be considered, particularly when the 'dilution solution' is pursued in relation to toxins. Indeed, societies creating substances which are either noxious or cannot be degraded or recycled should be drawn to conclude that they have failed.

Chinese successes in rural production without waste is firmly anchored to an observance of this stricture. Thus all synthetics should be branded harmful until proved benign. In particular, the biodegradability, harm-lessness and toleration properties of insecticides, pesticides, fungicides and herbicides must be demonstrated before their use is permitted. Likewise, fertilisers which combine with other substances to form toxins must be assessed; consumer durables must be manufactured in a way that allows eventual dismantling and recycling; and radioactive substances should only be used in small quantities under strict control.

A major problem in regulating the use of synthetic substances is defining how much is too much, and deciding how long the effects will persist. It is mainly because of the biologically unfavourable answers on both counts that DDT is roundly condemned in favour of the use of aldrin, dieldrin and chlorodane products.[14] Even so, the destruction caused by insecticides, pesticides and herbicides in the soil is still little considered. There may be ten micro-organisms in the top soil below a square metre of land, and this could be reduced by half through normal applications of 'acceptable' toxins. Yet, alarming though this may seem—who knows, and as nothing can be seen—who cares? It is in this context that DDT, employed mainly as an insecticide, comes in for a great deal of criticism. There is, on the one hand, its proven capability to reduce the amount of human misery here and now, but this has to be countered with a consideration of the inability of DDT to totally eradicate pests, and also its facility to allow the residual component of an insect population to survive and resist its use.[15] And as a direct result of DDT being used in such abundance to counter malaria, the populations of those countries carry the highest levels of its accumulation in body fats.

Lessons from experience

Satisfying the needs of an expanding human population must modify the

44

environment. The basic influences are threefold:

1 Some renewable resources are depleted at a greater rate than they are replenished.

2 Most non-renewable resources are dispersed too widely to be re-collected and re-used.

3 Residuals are discharged into some parts of the atmospheric and oceanic sinks beyond the rate at which they can be absorbed.

At base, ecodevelopment is concerned to conserve renewable resources, to pace or regulate the rate of exploitation of non-renewable resources and to control the discharge of residuals.

Urban and industrial artificiality works against these precepts, although the rate of resource use and residuals discharge would vary greatly between New York (where there are vast problems with toxins) and Calcutta (where wastes are largely biodegradable). Nevertheless, farming practice in the better off temperate zone, and a great deal of the plantation and larger scale farming in low income areas, relies upon mechanical and chemical inputs. The truth of the matter is that the impressive extant biomass in the humid tropical lands gives a misleading impression. These areas cannot produce sustained yields of essential grains for human consumption, despite mechanised and chemical farming, at rates that come anywhere near those obtainable in temperate lands. Large scale intensive agriculture in both the wet and arid tropics is a very complicated matter; economies of scale more often than not being cancelled out by the diseconomies of disaster. These points are now generally accepted; following Marsh's impressive lead in the last century, they were confirmed a hundred years later by Barbara Ward and René Dubos in their unofficial report to the Stockholm Conference on the Human Environment.[16] They highlight the complexities of nature's time clocks, energy triggers, storage facilities and reproduction mechanisms.

In some areas, most notably in Africa and the Amazon Basin, the low density of human population appears to grant a breathing space. Nature seems to be bountiful and extensive; why preach ecological harmony? Yet even within the bountiful continents the answer can be seen in Sahelian drought and Amazonian denudation.

The difficulty is that reharmonising altered ecosystems is now largely beyond the powers of direction because of the variables involved. The required harmony, which Ward and Dubos describe as 'a certain dynamic reciprocity', rests with human societies in their political planning capacities, for it is only at regional and national scales that the way human systems reciprocate with the resource endowment can be understood and effectively managed. There is no longer a mystery about the relationship of mankind to nature. Thus, in order to sustain dignified human life, it is necessary to condemn the materially advanced Northern nations for levels of consumption bound ultimately to lead to their own and everyone else's disenchantment. That is one matter; another is to ensure that the same path is not pursued in the poorer Southern world.

Rural and urban symbiosis also needs better understanding. When the resource chips are down the huge urban city of the tropics just might be a better place to live than the old world megalopolis, but only as the marginal better of two evils. It is all very well to postulate, as many do, that the city is the font of knowledge, erudition and innovation; but for what overall good or purpose in relation to transfixed, poverty stricken populations? Might not centres of 100,000 population perform the desired urban roles as well as the megalopolis, the needs of academics and culture seekers expected? Cities are worthy places to live for those who can utilise the access provided by the combustion of fossil fuels to get to what they want. Minus mobility and greenery they are rendered, from an ecological point of view, humanly invalid.

Much of the foregoing is probably acceptable in theory even if it is open to doubt in tactical terms. The technical problems involve deciding the level of 'carrying capacity' and determining the 'ecological thresholds' below which ecological damage reduces nutritional uptake and unacceptably impairs the human habitat. In fact, the two matters are closely related, for an important aspect of carrying capacity is that it represents the ecological threshold beyond which environmental qualities will deteriorate. It might be measured in terms of salinity introduced to an aquafer, an increase in biological oxygen demand in a river, particulate and gaseous content of the atmosphere, or a lowering of the microbiotic count in soils. Detection is more facile in some cases (river pollution) but it is fast becoming easier to monitor all environmental changes. Thus, given prognostications of carrying capacity, the Sahelian drought situation could have been foreseen; and in Peru the anchovy depletions could have been predicted, and so on. The point here is that it is now possible for valid technical recommendations to be made.

In nature there is, strictly, no such thing as an environmental crisis because nature always reacts to restore an equilibrium. Thus, the global ecosystem is simply what mankind in societies fashion it to be. Expressed in another way, a polluted environment with lowered ecological diversity is a platform which people make and on which they must reside. Societies must express the quality of life they are prepared to settle for in relation to available resources; in short, establishing an equilibrium requires the pre-establishment of critical ecological thresholds.

The tropics present a few special advantages and disadvantages as a platform for human habitation. Nobody in their right mind would prefer

Canada as a physical environment to the Canaries, or Moscow to the Marquesas. The tropics saw the birth of mankind, and the evidence is that they are the most suitable human habitat. Nevertheless, the delicacy and diversity of tropical ecosystems, and their sensitivity to change, render them complex. Even for agriculture regulated with every caution, the production of the most important staple foods (rice, wheat and corn) are below the levels of production per field worker in temperate areas. This pattern is not much improved when output is considered in terms of production per hectare because of the greater demand for plant support which crops make in the tropics. Furthermore, mankind is getting at tropical resources with awesome efficacy. The rapid increase in the means of access on land, over water and in the air are supplemented by indirect methods of data assembly from aerial photography and satellite imagery. These facilitate relatively effortless exploitation. And, having got to the resource, another set of technological powers are used. These include earth moving machinery for land clearing and irrigation, the application of chemical controls, biological interventions, and the use of fertilisers and plant genetics—all very abrasive in the tropical context. Never in the history of mankind has so much physical power been available, but nowhere in the world can this lead more quickly to disaster than between Cancer and Capricorn. A call arises for an understanding of 'political ecology', a social-science-come-natural-science hybrid concerned with economic well being, social fairness and environmental equilibrium.

Notes

1   Keith C. Barrons, *The Food in Your Future,* Reinhold, New York, 1975, p.173.

2   Max Nicholson, *The Environmental Revolution,* Hodder and Stoughton, London, 1970; E.P. Eckholm, *Losing Ground,* Norton, New York, 1976.

3   Various distinctions are possible. I prefer that made by A.S. Travis in a paper 'New Directions in Rural and Natural Science Resource Management', *Proceedings of the Town Planning Summer School,* St Andrews, September 1972. Travis conceptualised inherited human artefacts and heritages as 'extrinsic' resources.

4   For a definitive survey, see F.M. Peterson and A.C. Fisher, 'The Exploitation of Extractive Resources', *The Economic Journal,* no.348, December 1977, pp.681—721.

5   Well detailed by C.D. Idyll, 'The Anchovy Crisis', *Scientific American,* reprint no.1273, June, 1973.

6   United Nations Environmental Programme, *Report of the Executive Director,* Governing Council Address, Nairobi, April 1975. (UNEP/GC/30 — mimeographed.)

7   Erik P. Eckholm, *Losing Ground,* Morton, New York, 1976, p.120.

8   Gerald Foley has written something scientific, but not obtuse in his book *The Energy Question,* Penguin, London, 1976, which would interest those wishing to delve more fully into the matter of energy balance. The workings of metabolism are also well expressed from the broader ecological rather than the narrower biological viewpoint by P.R. Ehrlich, A.H. Ehrlich and J.P. Holdren, *Ecoscience,* Freeman, San Francisco, 1977.

9   Foley (ibid, p.39) observes that: 'The efficiency with which the biosphere converts solar energy to organic matter is in general very low. Under optimum conditions 2 per cent of the visible radiation may be used, but more usually it is only a fraction of this . . . about a fifth of one per cent. About a third of the photosynthetic production occurs in the seas and oceans; the rest occurs on land.'

10   The full list runs: (a) producers; (b) primary consumers; (c) secondary and tertiary consumers (such as lions that eat antelope, and lice that live on lions) and (d) decomposers (such as worms and bacteria).

11   An excellent review of the subject in more detail is undertaken by Odum under the sub-heading 'Food Chains, Food Webs and Trophic Levels', Eugene P. Odum, *Fundamentals of Ecology* (third edition), Saunders, Philadelphia, 1971, p.63.

12   For more detail refer to Richard H.V. Bell, 'A Grazing Ecosystem in the Serengeti', *Scientific American,* (offprint no.1228), July 1971.

13   Alan Cottrell (Sir), *Environmental Economics,* Edward Arnold, London, 1978, p.42.

14   A full catalogue of modern control chemicals includes: inorganic pesticides, botanicals (plant extracts), chlorinated hydrocarbons, organophosphorous compounds, carbonates, fossil oils, mercury compounds, antibiotics, phenal derivatives, organic acids, anticoagulants. Refer to C. and P. ReVelle, *Sourcebook on the Environment,* Houghton Mifflin, Boston, 1974.

15   Articles that argue respectively for and against the use of DDT are: (a) M.J. Grayson and T.R. Shepard, *The Disaster Lobby,* chapter 2, Follet, Chicago, 1973; and (b) Richard Garcia, 'The control of Malaria', *Environment,* vol.14, no.5, June 1972.

16   Barbara Ward and René Dubos, *Only One Earth,* Andre Deutsch, London, 1972.

3 Human factor proportions

> No civilisation prior to the European had occasion
> to believe in the systematic material progress of the
> whole human race; no civilisation drove itself
> relentlessly to an ever-receding goal; no civilisation
> was too passion-charged to replace what is with
> what could be; no civilisation had striven as the
> West has done to direct the world according to its
> will; no civilisation has known so few moments of
> peace and tranquility.
>
> *W. Woodruff, 1967*[1]

Attempts to locate a definition of low income nations prove largely
futile. Finite measurements of gross national product and energy consumption give valid statistical signposts to a general understanding;
but the environment in which human beings live is a complex multi-
dimensional 'system' which defies compartmenting. Diagram 8 is a
representation of the way these nations articulate, but mainly from a
growth perspective.[2] In fact, with such complex systems no established
discipline, and certainly no scholar, can claim to completely understand
what it is all about.[3] It can therefore be argued that it is no more possible
or indeed necessary to have a complete understanding of the workings
of political ecology than it is to fully comprehend the concept of
infinity or that of the beginning of time. Nevertheless, disciplines
structure communities of knowledge into assimilable parts. It is in this
way, but from a monetary platform, that political economy works to

This diagram is a representation of the relationship between land, mankind and what has loosely been shown as the development system. Reality is much more complicated than the schema shown opposite, but here I came up against two constraints; first, the basic need to express political ecology as an aid to overall understanding; and second, the technical limitation to modelling on the printed page.

(a) This construct fits those economies that have been associated with the forms of economic growth where mankind controls nature, particularly in the Northern nations. It still works well for them and it has worked well in the past for those privileged by military and economic advantage to wield power (Europe), the zealously industrious (Japan) and those at the resource frontier (the New World)—but this is only one sixth of the world population! Later I will attempt to show that the syndrome manifested here has little to commend it in poor nations where mankind is more at the mercy of nature and each nation suffers economic isolation.

(b) Land (the biosphere) is fundamental in the representation because mankind cannot exist without it. For an economist, land is not held to be more important than the other factors (labour and capital) of production.

(c) The economists' trinity (land, labour and capital) might assign labour here.

(d) A 'development system' is a set of institutions devised to allocate and use resources through institutional networks. Planning systems are sub-parts of development systems. The level of development attained is a function of the power structure, the subject of the next chapter.

(e) Increasing consumption and prosperity are shown here as outputs from positive development; reality for low income countries frequently leads to reduced *per capita* consumption and austerity.

(f) Pollution can be the result of inadequately controlled technology and need not be directly related to high-consumption—but in poorer areas such controls are usually absent. The depletion of non-renewable (mineral) resources is inevitable. The problem of renewable resources (soils, water, flora and fauna) lies at the heart of political ecology.

(g) Population increase is no longer an outcome of prosperity in the rich nations, but it certainly remains as an outcome of significance in low income nations.

(h) Capital varies from scarcity to excess even within low income countries.

(i) Unskilled labour (reflected as underemployment and unemployment) is widely available, although many operational skills may be in short supply.

(j) Technology can be viewed in two ways. Some countries seek to avoid technological dependence by going it alone (characterised by 'soft' appropriate technology); and others a technological fix (characterised by the use of 'hard' imported technology).

(k) Few low income nations have much secondary production, one of the main elements of conflict in the North-South dialogue.

(l) Food (2,200—2,700 calories per day), adequate clothing and appropriate shelter.

(m) The line between physical health and ill-health is usually measured in terms of fitness to work; and a reduction in this rate is consequent upon nutritional uptake and the preventative and curative components in public health programmes.

(n) Recognition of status, access to privacy, freedom of expression, guarantee of rights, and freedom from arbitrary arrest contribute to psychological wellbeing.

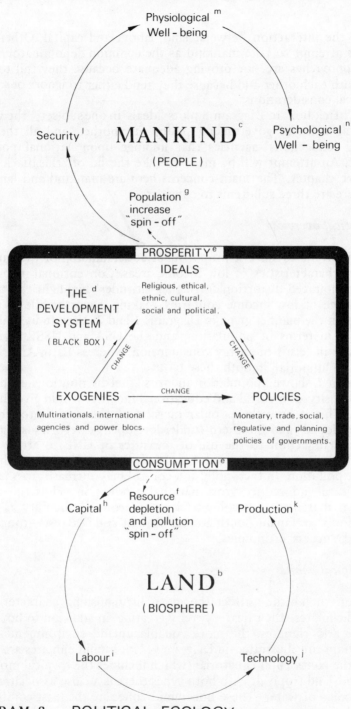

Physiological [m]
Well - being

Security [l]　　MANKIND [c]　　Psychological [n]
Well - being
(PEOPLE)

Population [g]
increase
"spin - off"

PROSPERITY [e]

IDEALS

THE [d]
DEVELOPMENT
SYSTEM
Religious, ethical,
ethnic, cultural,
social and political.

(BLACK BOX)

CHANGE　　CHANGE

EXOGENIES　　CHANGE　　POLICIES

Multinationals, international
agencies and power blocs.
Monetary, trade, social,
regulative and planning
policies of governments.

CONSUMPTION [e]

Capital [h]　　Resource [f]
depletion
and pollution
"spin - off"
Production [k]

LAND [b]
(BIOSPHERE)

Labour [i]　　Technology [j]

DIAGRAM 8　　POLITICAL ECOLOGY :
MAN, LAND AND DEVELOPMENT [a]

explain the interaction between land, labour and capital. Other social sciences attempt to take mankind as the common denominator. Today these approaches are not proving adequate because they fail to inter-relate with each other and because they tend either to ignore or set aside ecological considerations.

The 'black box' in Diagram 8 plots 'ideals' in one sub-set,[4] the within-nation agencies of government 'policy' in another, and all the inter-national 'exogenous' agencies that impinge upon national policy in another. An attempt will be made to take the lid off this black box in the next chapter. The main concerns here are mankind and land—but first there are three sub-items to consider.

A statistical overview

It is important to have a proportional understanding of the bulk and location characteristics of low income areas. Conventional maps (with their pronounced distortion for higher latitudes) highlight the tropical prominence of low income countries, making it worthwhile to redraw the map in the manner given in Diagrams 1 and 2. Here India and China dominate in terms of population, and the USA and USSR register as impressive in terms of energy consumption, whereas Latin America and Africa are lilliputian in both these terms.

Diagram 1 showed population and fossil fuel distributions. Depictions of the density of medical and educational facilities would give the same picture. This is how the popular division of the world into Northern (overdeveloped) and Southern (underdeveloped) categories is made. An important objection to the use of measures of GNP to arrive at this form of economic pecking order is that it fails to incorporate the price paid for pollution. In fact, pollution control may increase gross national expenditure and reduce gross national production. Thus the cost of pollution abatement can come back as an economic liability as is now well known in Japan, South Korea, Taiwan and Malaysia—four highly polluted 'success' economies.

The tropical habitat

Variations in altitude affect the most distinguishing characteristic of tropical climates—their heat—thereby creating, in addition to hot-humid and hot-arid climates, the more equable upland environments. These distinctions are illustrated in Diagram 9. Hot-humid climates are of two kinds: the continental equatorial (which includes the tropical monsoon) and the island tropical. With both types there is a close association with large bodies of water. These hot-humid zones are the least comfortable tropical climates for human existence simply because it is not practicable to bring about an efficient heat exchange in a cloudy, humid and windless

52

atmosphere. Water borne diseases are endemic. Hot-arid climates are characteristic of areas away from the equator. Maximum temperatures are generally hotter than body temperature; but the diurnal range is also greater and nights are therfore cool. The contrast between seasons is also more noticeable. Human comfort is more easily attained in hot-arid climates than in the humid tropics. Dust borne diseases are prevalent. Tropical upland climates are characterised by marked daily variations in temperature. Ground frosts may occur on cold nights. The attainment of human comfort is more a problem of adjusting to the extremes of cold than the extremes of heat. Tropical upland climates are healthy and physiologically acceptable as an environment for human existence.

The factor proportions

The usual way to classify factor proportions in low income countries is in accordance with a topology which embraces agriculture, industry and services—the primary, secondary, tertiary sectors. Data of these kinds are difficult to interpret because of difficulties in establishing a clear and common definition for each sector, and of detecting the employment role of women, known to be dominant in the primary sector. Nor is it usually possible to break each sector into different kinds of primary, secondary and tertiary occupations in accordance with the nine significant employment groups identified by the International Labour Office.[6] Here we are concerned with political ecology, and such an environmentally determined matter, linked to the basic outline of resources and ecology given in the previous chapter, highlights mankind and land as the fundamental factor proportions; and it is to a consideration of these that we now turn.

Mankind (see Diagram 8)

Marx observed that 'nature fixed in isolation from man is nothing for man',[7] a truism with a corollary, namely that people are also a product of their environment: thus mankind considered apart from land has no meaning. It is from this pragmatic understanding that people, as factors for production, can be assessed in terms of population numbers and production potential.

Demographic structure

The population density per square kilometre for most nations is shown in Diagram 10. The information relates to countries, not geographical regions. A closer examination of this diagram in relation to Diagram 1

Although low income countries do not necessarily lie between the tropics of Capricorn and Cancer, that is where they generally arise. The most healthy of these climates are the tropical uplands, the least healthy are the hot humid areas. Climate is very significant in terms of human comfort and greatly influences building design; hence the thick walled, heavily roofed, dense housing of the dry areas and the flimsy, lightly roofed, well spaced housing of the wet areas.

	HOT HUMID	HOT ARID	TROPICAL UPLAND
HUMIDITY			
Absolute Humidity	18 – 30 millibars	7 – 15 mb / 15 – 20 during rains	Dry Season 8–12mb/Wet 12–16mb
Relative Humidity	High: 55 – 100%	Low: 10 – 55% (lower inland)	45 – 100%
RAINFALL			
Annual	Usually exceeds 1250 mm	Usually less than 250 mm	Variable–Typically below 1000 mm
Monthly	Usually exceeds 50 mm	Usually less than 50 mm	Marked dry and wet season
SHADE TEMPERATURE			
Maximum	Rarely exceeds 32°C	Usually exceeds 32°C	26°C at 1800 m
Minimum	21 – 26°C	14 – 21°C	10 – 15°C (Frosts may form)
Diurnal Range	5 – 9°C	12 – 22°C	11 – 17°C
SKY	Usually cloudy	Usually clear	Clear or partly cloudy
WIND MOVEMENT	Generally slight	Often strong	Variable according to topography
EXAMPLES	**FREETOWN**	**KHARTOUM**	**NAIROBI** El. 1820 m.

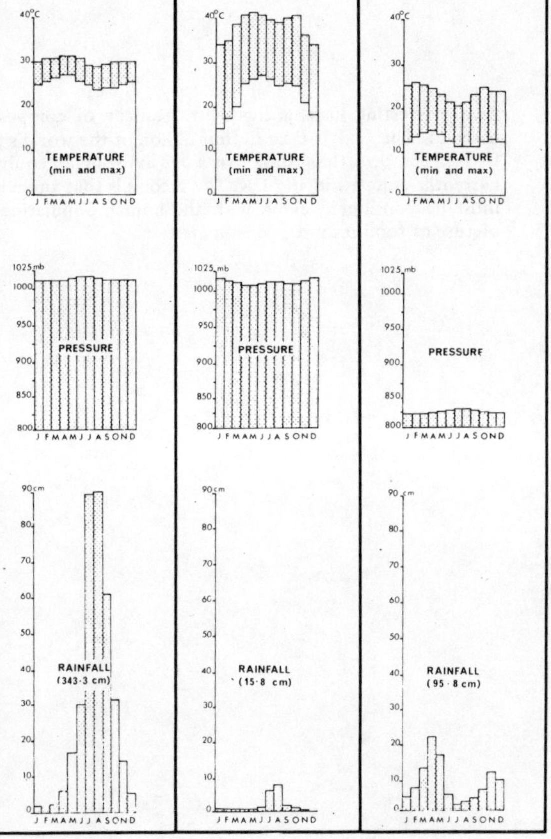

DIAGRAM 9
GENERAL CHARACTERISTICS OF TROPICAL CLIMATES

55

Two interesting insights highlight a fallacy of composition in this diagram. The first is that all four billion of the world's people could fit into the USA (less Alaska) at a density roughly equivalent to that currently enjoyed in the UK. The second is that animals of all kinds must be considered along with the human population in the total picture of food resource consumers.

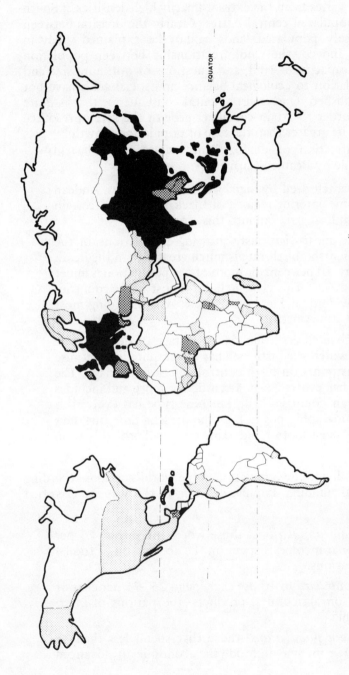

POPULATION PER SQUARE KILOMETER*

	0 – 10
	11 – 30
	31 – 70
	71 +

*Densities averaged within the boundaries of each country.

EQUATOR

DIAGRAM 10

57

discloses that there is a range of population densities throughout the poor nations that varies from the extraordinarily high densities of South Asia to sparsely populated central Africa. Clearly the division between densely and sparsely populated lands cannot be explained solely in terms of climate. Indeed, the whole relationship between population and the carrying capacity of land, and questions of optimum size and growth rate in relation to ecological balance and social goals have not been clearly established. One environmental consequence that is quite certain is that in order to attain consumer growth the rate of resource exploitation must be greater than the rate of population growth.[8]

A useful classification of demographic classes which has proved durable is that made by Beaujeu-Garnier.[9]

1 *Primitive*—characterised by high birth and death rates. Andean countries, some interior regions of black Africa, and certain parts of South East Asia fall into this group.

2 *Youthful*—the most vigorously growing populations in the world, in which the birth rate is much greater than the death rate and where 40 per cent or more of the population is under fifteen years of age. This class includes almost all the countries of Africa, the Middle East and Eastern Asia including most countries in Latin America.

3 *Mature*—which includes countries at a stage of demographic evolution in which the birth rate has fallen quite low because of social constraints on birth control and late marriage. The normal type has evolved over a century or more and includes most European countries. The Japanese type has evolved to the same demographic position at the present time but their evolution has been more rapid. This class will probably soon include China.

It is also useful to divide the population of the world's nations according to their nutritional standing. Populations can, in this way, be classified as:

1 *High food drain populations*—those where more than 75 per cent of personal income is spent on the acquisition of food—the poorest nations.

2 *Transitional populations*—those that spend 25–75 per cent of their income on agricultural products—the nations of intermediate income.

3 *Low food drain populations*—those that spend less than 25 per cent of their income on food—the economically advanced nations.

There has been some success in the move toward food self-sufficiency in Japan; China with nearly a quarter of the world's population is achieving wonders and India, the most populous mixed economy nation is enjoying limited success.

The recent age compositions for the three countries given in Diagram 11 (one nation from each part of the low income tricontinent) show the youthful bases which underline the potential for similar but even larger populations. At the same time, it also suggests future unemployment problems. Add to this the fact that half the people in low income countries are malnourished because of the denial of essential nutrients and that a quarter are undernourished in relation to standard calorie requirements, then the picture of population growth as a major problem becomes terrifyingly clear.

Population growth

World population is growing exponentially. The total today is four billions; 45 years ago it was two billions, and 80 years before that it was one billion. The surge arose this century because of lower infant mortality and greater longevity. Crude birth and death rate data for Sri Lanka has demonstrated the influence of a vigorous public health campaign against malaria and, more recently, the effects of limited birth control measures. This can also be seen in Table 3 in terms of the rates of overall population increase. The correlation between high rates of population increase and intermediate country status is clearly established; and likewise a correlation between poverty and lower rates of population increase (more births, but coupled to earlier deaths) is also apparent. Poor nations compound their population problem when they pursue comprehensive health programmes concerned with curative and preventive medicine.

Migration

Migration is of two kinds, between national territories and within the boundaries of a nation. The spread of people into the current low income regions involved the movement of Europeans (now a relatively minor proportion of permanent settlers in the tropical lands); twenty million Chinese to South East Asia, Indonesia and the Philippines; Syrians and Lebanese to black Africa; Africans to the Central Americas; ten million Indians to Malaysia, Southern Africa, the West Indies, Fiji and Mauritius; and three million Japanese to Hawaii, Peru and Brazil. On moving, these people were severed from the cultural security of their homelands and, as might be expected, they adapted and profited from economic opportunity more quickly than local populations until today, in most of the countries listed, they represent the commercial

The most usual ascription to data of this kind is that half the population is under fifteen years of age. The population dynamics involved are such that a seventy year old person lives in a world that is four times as populated as it was at the time of his or her birth.

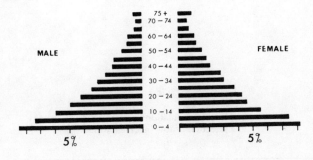

PERU

MALE

FEMALE

75 +
70 − 74
60 − 64
50 − 54
40 − 44
30 − 34
20 − 24
10 − 14
0 − 4

5%   5%

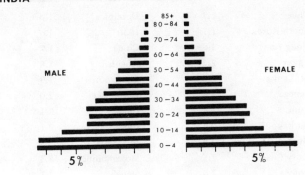

INDIA

MALE

FEMALE

85+
80 − 84
70 − 74
60 − 64
50 − 54
40 − 44
30 − 34
20 − 24
10 − 14
0 − 4

5%   5%

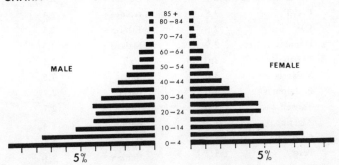

GHANA

MALE

FEMALE

85+
80 − 84
70 − 74
60 − 64
50 − 54
40 − 44
30 − 34
20 − 24
10 − 14
0 − 4

5%   5%

AGE AND SEX COMPOSITION
PERU, INDIA AND GHANA

DIAGRAM 11

Table 3

Mean annual rate of population increase (% 1974—1978)
in a selection of low income nations

Intermediate countries (ranked)		Poor countries (ranked)	
Chile	1.7	Dominica	1.0
South Korea	1.7	Haiti	1.6
Hong Kong	1.8	China	1.7
Egypt	2.2	Angola	1.8
Sri Lanka	2.3	Cameroon	1.9
Senegal	2.4	Burundi	2.0
Tunisia	2.4	Chad	2.1
Turkey	2.4	India	2.1
Guatemala	2.5	Indonesia	2.3
Ivory Coast	2.5	Mozambique	2.3
Bolivia	2.6	Nepal	2.3
Ghana	2.7	Upper Volta	2.3
Morocco	2.7	Afghanistan	2.4
North Korea	2.7	Burma	2.4
Brazil	2.8	Guinea	2.4
Iran	2.8	Ethiopia	2.5
Dominican Rep.	2.9	Malawi	2.5
El Salvador	3.0	Mali	2.5
Malaysia	3.0	Sudan	2.5
Philippines	3.0	Niger	2.7
Taiwan	3.0	Tanzania	2.7
Algeria	3.2	Cambodia	2.8
Colombia	3.2	Congo	3.1
Peru	3.2	Yemen	3.1
Iraq	3.3	Thailand	3.2
Syria	3.3	Pakistan	3.3
Zambia	3.3	Uganda	3.3
Ecuador	3.4		

elite. These former migrants are almost entirely urban living peoples. Despite undercurrents of discontent from the original inhabitants, their presence is well established.

More recent international migrants are not yet settled. In the poorer parts of the world the greatest upheaval resulted from the partition which created Pakistan upon the independence of India in 1947—a movement of more than seventeen million people. The end of the British mandate for the new state of Israel attracted enormous numbers of immigrants and created a lesser countermigration of Arab people. The pre-war population of Hong Kong had doubled to three million people by 1960, due predominantly to the inflow of refugees from mainland China. Most recently, some four millions have been displaced in Kampuchea. Africa has experienced the flight into the Ibo heartland, the Ugandan exodus and migration due to drought.

The many causes which bring about population movements of this order include economic, personal, family, community, health, political, religious, ethnic and even psychological factors. Such lists are confusing because the lesser attractions (toward bright lights) appear to be of equal importance to the major repellents (flight for safety). In the same way, the movement to the cities generates spectacular urban problems (such as distortion of the sex ratio and a demand for housing as well as schools and hospitals) which obscure the more critical problems of reduced agricultural production as a result of the outward migration of the active work force.

Health and nutrition

Low productivity is linked to undernourishment and ill-health, but the complexity of comparability tempts one to claim that no universal indicator of nutritional need exists for people of different kinds in different climates. However, the general situation is:

1 That the well nourished nations are, with minor exceptions, wholly outside the tropical zones.

2 That most of the peoples of Africa and Central and South America have marginally adequate food intakes (2,200—2,700 calories per day).

3 That the principal location of undernourished people is tropical and sub-tropical Asia.

Nutritional sufficiency is obviously reflected in national productivity, and raising food intake has been a cornerstone of many national development plans.

Specific nutrition correlated diseases such as beri-beri, pellagra and rickets are easily identified, but there is a wider range of pathological disorders where a correlation between nutritional deficiency and the incidence of disease can be shown. The most significant are tuberculosis, typhus, malaria and intestinal diseases. The swamp diseases can be checked and in the case of malaria, the most widespread tropical disease, largely eliminated by a combination of drainage control and chemotherapy; intestinal diseases and tuberculosis can be kept down by improvements in public sanitation and home hygiene; the clearance of forest undercover can eliminate the tsetse fly and thence sleeping sickness; and immunological innoculation can check the incidence of many of the remaining tropical diseases and disorders.

The rate of incidence and the period of debility for the nutrition correlated disorders can be reduced by improving food intake, which means increasing the bulk and raising the quality of foodstuffs. This in turn requires improved land management. This condition is clearly illustrated by comparing land utilisation in the low density Congo and Amazon basins with the agriculture of the high density Red River delta where a pattern of ecologically efficient agriculture has been practised for millennia. Care must be taken over the definition of efficiency because figures relating to inputs are not always comparable. Paterson's comparison of rice growing in China and the USA illustrates the point.

> In China, the yield is a little over one ton to the acre, and in the USA about half as much again. But the input mix in the two cases is utterly different: in the Chinese situation, the labour of one man produces little more than an acre of rice in each growing season, while in the USA, where he is aided by aeroplanes and tractors with balloon tyres, one operator can farm 80 to 100 acres. The labour input in America is therefore only one eightieth that of the Chinese. But this discrepancy is, of course, balanced by different inputs of the additional factor—capital (in the form of fossil fuels). For many Asian rice cultivators, 'capital' means simply their seed, one or two hand tools and a right to use water. An American rice farmer, on the other hand, is encouraged . . . to consider, as a 'reasonable equipment inventory for a medium sized farm', two tractors, a truck, two breaking ploughs, a disc harrow, a section harrow, a grader, a roller, a drill, a combine and a grain cart, as well as 60 to 140 pounds of chemical fertilisers to the acre. The astonishing thing is that, at the end of the day, such different inputs should yield so nearly comparable results.[10]

Whilst the comparability of rates of production per acre are apparent, factor proportions determine that these results are reached by completely different routes. Also, of course, if the two systems of rice growing were accounted for in separate energy budgets then the non-renewable fossil fuel 'price' of rice in the USA would be much more 'costly' than in China. Yet another important twist is that the equipment cost per agricultural workplace (this time in monetary terms) might, even excluding land costs, differ 100 to 1 from $10,000 in the USA to $100 in China.

The use of preventative medical technology to promote productivity by curing the diseases which retard economic expansion, and the use of birth limitation to regulate population growth are means by which the poverty cycle can be broken; but the first problem is less one of international resources than of the need for decisions about the worth of human numbers and the desirability of goods.

Land (Diagram 8)

The resources of the endowment platform are fundamental to human existence. Soils, minerals, water and solar incidence have been examined in the previous chapter. Now, as land types, the resource endowment platform can be considered as comprising: (a) open areas (mainly rural but including open water), and (b) man made urban and infrastructural forms.

Open areas

The use of open land can be viewed in three main ways: as a resource to conserve, to preserve or exploit. Conservation requires the balanced use of resources continuously; preservation implies leaving some resources untouched; exploitation relates mainly to mineral, fish and timber abstraction for profit, but there are also forms of agricultural and pastoral exploitation that result either in soil exhaustion or soil resource depletion.

Extractive mineral industries are an economic lynchpin for many low income countries. A short list of the more important examples would include oil exploitation in the Middle East, Central America, West Africa and the East Indies; copper mining in Chile, Central Africa and Papua New Guinea; gold and diamond mining in West Africa; iron ore mining in India, Sierra Leone, Venezuela and Brazil, and tin mining in Malaysia, Burma and Bolivia. The extent to which it is appropriate to judge the extraction of these non-renewable resources as extortionate and exploitative is a function of royalty payments, control over waste discharges (particularly toxins) and the degree of land restoration. Mineral exploitation, never a subtle activity, has become relatively more savage in the postwar era with both the host countries and the Northern 'developers' pursuing their own forms of extortion—maximum royalties and minimum expenditure—to limits that are not in the interests of stabilising incomes, employment or the rate of abstraction. The extent to which low income countries attempt to utilise the short term revenues generated through the exploitation of mineral resources in order to ease the annual budget along, rather than to prime long term development programmes, does little more than store up problems for the future.

Subsistence farming (which includes pastoral nomadism) is a method of agriculture mostly characterised by a rotation of cultivated spaces (or grazing ranges) without the aid of irrigation—'land use rotation' rather than a rotation of crops.[11] Only twelve to twenty people can live on a square kilometre under these conditions, and shortening the period of rotation (ideally twenty-four years in fallow) results in reduced yields. The introduction of improved hand tools, and sedentary bush fallowing, can only marginally increase yields. This system of farming must be seen, therefore, to be ecologically adaptive and resource sustaining but inadequate for supporting a dense population; hence wherever the practice is widespread it will not support the growth of industry or urbanisation. Because of this it is the most widely condemned agricultural practice in the tropics. Subsistence populations are thus often accused of depressing the living standard because of their net abstraction from social services, when in most cases people living at subsistence levels could be regarded as being innocently and blessedly self-sufficient and in ecological balance; neither contributing to, nor substantially taking from, national finance.

Smallhold farming in tropical and sub-tropical areas is characterised by low *per capita* and per unit area productivity (relative to intensive smallhold farming in temperate areas); but advantages over subsistence production in land use, rotation of crops, and mixed husbandry, can be detected. Quite successful patterns of smallhold farming can be observed in the semi-rural lands surrounding large urban centres in most low income countries. Smallhold pastoralism was rather unusual prior to European influence because of the absence of suitable animals to rear (South America), the prevalence of animal diseases (Africa and Asia) and the low nutrient value of tropical grasslands. Now, however, smallhold pastoralism flourishes.

Smallhold mixed farming, which is a blend of cultivation and stock raising, is still sadly lacking. Often animals are regarded as beasts of burden, or as objects of wealth or veneration. The value of fish as a source of protein for consumption, like the worth of animal manure for soil fertilisation, is still badly neglected. Although smallhold farming is somewhat inefficient in absolute terms, it is here, rather than in subsistence farming, that improved agricultural practices can be assimilated and a direct beneficial effect upon cropping can be obtained.

Plantation production is a system of agriculture linked historically with the most abhorred institution of human domination—slavery. Yet to associate plantation agriculture with slavery alone can be misleading. One aftermath of the early application of the plantation system has been its contribution of a systematised and effective tropical agriculture, a feature well illustrated in contemporary times in the Gezira area of the Sudan, the sugar production areas of north east Brazil, and tea production in Sri Lanka. The problem of the present is how, in independent tropical countries, to overcome the understandable prejudice against the plantation system and avoid the vulnerability of monoculture, yet retain the technical heritage of efficient plantation management. Here is where co-operative farming can offer an answer.

Fish farming from inland ponds and marine farming from continental shelves are forms of protein production that can exceed the conventional production from grazing herbivores.[12] In the previous chapter the catalogue of disasters, environmental and human induced, which drastically affected the Peruvian anchovy industry signposts the need for caution. Nevertheless, the extension of fishing to the underused parts of continental shelves (marine farming) together with the detection of deep water upwellings and their exploitation (fish harvesting) could raise the total yield from 60 million tons (1980) to 200 million tons a year. International agreement and effective regulation of catching practices and marine pollution are the key problems to be overcome.

Forestry practice in humid Asia and much of humid Africa has generally become exploitative, but note that the formerly marketable species have made up only a very small portion (about 1 per cent) of the large trees in these forest areas. The variety of trees coupled to technical difficulties in the use of tropical timbers, particularly for paper manufacture, has resulted in spatially extensive exploitation that has left ecological devastation in its wake.[13] There is great potential to be gained from improved forest management, but it should also be remembered that silviculture in the tropics remains more difficult and less practical than in temperate areas, and requires capable and sustained management. Plantation forestry in the semi-arid zones, the savannas that were originally forest areas, is a possibility, but a main objective with forestry in these areas is generally to improve local environmental conditions.

Agricultural efficiency. Agricultural efficiency might be measured in terms of monetary profits, unit area production, energy use, or worker output; efficiency in all cases being:

$$\frac{\text{output}}{\text{input}}$$

usually expressed as a percentage. When resources are abundant, or the currency stable, an output of monetary profits over investment inputs is seen as an expression of efficiency.

67

This diagram is redrawn from information supplied from correspondence with Gerald Leach, and his text, *Energy and Food Production*. An interesting supplementary fact is that the fossil fuel inputs to agriculture in the economically advanced countries are a small proportion (4.6 per cent in the UK) of the national consumption of fossil based energy: suggesting, in turn, that it is in industry, transportation and domestic energy consumption that greater energy savings can most easily be made.

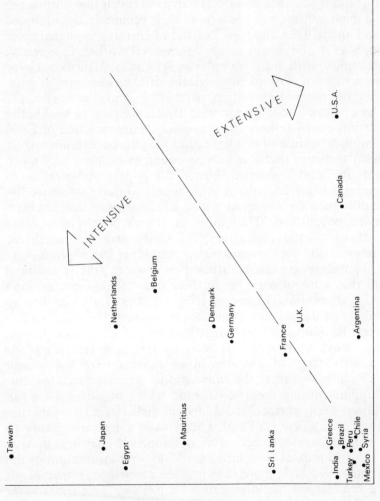

OUTPUT per WORKER expressed as Wheat - Equivalent Units

DIAGRAM 12 AGRICULTURAL OUTPUTS

Gerald Leach shows, in *Energy and Food Production*, just how efficient, in terms of fuel energy inputs to food energy outputs, the subsistence, pre-industrial and Chinese farming systems are when compared with industrial farming systems.[14] Diagram 12, redrawn from Leach, illustrates a pattern whereby the unit area intensiveness of agriculture in some countries is shown between 12 o'clock and 1:30, as it were, on the diagram; and unit area extensiveness is shown for other countries between 1:30 and 3 o'clock. But this is not all, for near the horizontal axis of the graph is shown a close correlation between low output per hectare and high output per worker in such economically advanced countries as Canada, USA and New Zealand where it is known that there is also a high level of investment per agricultural worker. Conversely, the diagram shows, with such examples as Sri Lanka, Mauritius, Egypt and Taiwan which are close to the vertical axis, the close correlation in these contexts between high output per hectare and low output per worker. There is not enough underused land or capital to enable the Northern nation model to be applied in Asia, Africa or much of Latin America; and it is because of this limitation plus the condemning effect of population increases that low income countries cannot easily move to the right on Leach's diagram. Hence the popular exhortation to increase production per hectare, in other words to move up vertically. This is the only path for countries where all the useable land has been given over to production. Thus most of the densely settled Asian countries, of which the Philippines, Sri Lanka and Bangladesh are typical examples, can work toward higher output per area of production rather than pursuing increased output per worker. This is a dismal posture and thus a frequent prayer in these countries is for some kind of technological solution. Higher yielding varieties (HYV) leading to the so-called Green Revolution is one such movement.

The Green Revolution began with the breeding of a high yielding dwarf maize stock in Mexico that took up fertilisers effectively and tolerated a wide range of climates. More important for low income areas was Chandler's work at the International Rice Research Institute in the Philippines during the 1960 decade which produced IR–8, an Asian crossbred strain of rice that doubled the yields from local varieties. The introduction of new HYVs of wheat made a dramatic change to food output in India; rice remained more important elsewhere in Asia. But in fact the additional food made available for consumption in the hungry countries did little more than provide a welcome improvement, and merely represented the buying of a little time. There could never be any moral grounds for not taking up the higher yielding varieties, but they strew in their wake many disturbing issues such as the heavy demands they made on fossil fuel based fertilisers. More importantly, the HYVs of the 1970s must not be allowed to create a population explosion in the 1980s, particularly as the introduction of singularly successful monospecies in intensive monoculture increases the likelihood of crop failure on a big scale.

These HYVs respond well to fertiliser application and it is twice as gainful to use fertilisers on HYV crops in poorer nations than on the already overenriched croplands of the economically advanced countries. But as these fertiliser inputs are largely fossil fuel based where, in future, are they to come from? A further practical problem is that production from HYV stock calls for more lavish applications of pesticides and insecticides than was first envisaged, and these costs must also be entered on the balance sheet of gains and losses. There is the further fact that the 'economies of scale' argument for better profits leads generally to capital intense mechanisation.

Productivity and efficiency in agriculture is as much related to management as to farming technique. Furthermore, for the tropics generally, soils are deficient in humus and assimilable minerals. These observations are reflected in Table 4 which illustrates the relative inefficiency of agriculture in the tropical countries, although there are also differing levels of aptitude and technological input to take into account. The net result in terms of the globally most important crop—wheat—is shown in Table 5. Here the importance of North America as the breadbasket of the world can be noted. Food as aid is thus an important example of the way in which externalities affect political ecology because food as aid will, in the absence of related birth limitation policies, cause a population to be nutritionally better equipped to produce more children faster, thereby exacerbating and prolonging the very nutritional problem it is intended to allay. It has, for example, been established that food aid to India (the major recipient) has induced a breakdown in the internal system for local marketing, which in turn has caused grain to accumulate at the farm gate and ultimately has undermined production in drought free years where self-sufficiency might have been attained. Food distribution for strictly humanitarian reasons in cases of nutritional severity will always cause governments to be moved to provide assistance ; but food distribution as a surplus disposal mechanism is unconscionable. Setting aside humanitarian niceties, the only really tenable long term posture is for hungry nations to technically improve their own production capabilities.

Higher yielding varieties have been seen as a production fix for Asia whereas the solution employed to boost food production in Africa and South America has been the pursuit of new lands policies. But in all these countries it is important that the food producing capacity be used to calculate the human population that can be nourished. This involves a political choice—consumption goods or basic foodstuffs. In the densely populated poor countries it is clearly a matter of food first, although the ruling elite will often see priorities differently. There is no production fix. In this assessment, plant breeding leading to fertiliser demands which

Table 4

Yield of principal crops

	Europe	North America	South America	Asia	Africa	Oceania
Wheat	1980	1640	1630	860	800	1400
Rye	1840	1190	850	1040	440	500
Barley	2680	1870	1230	960	670	1400
Oats	1940	1570	1300	1240	490	910
Maize	2510	3070	1360	1150	1080	2220
Paddy rice	4650	3220	1530	1830	1780	4860
Cotton lint	410	600	260	190	260	–

Source: Benjamin Higgins, *Economic Development*

Table 5

The world grain trade

	1960	1966	1973
	(million metric tons)		
North America	+ 39	+ 59	+ 91
Australasia	+ 6	+ 8	+ 6
Europe and USSR	– 25	– 31	– 46
Latin America	0	+ 5	– 3
Africa	– 2	– 7	– 9
Asia	– 17	– 34	– 43

(Based on US Department of Agriculture figures, 1974)

cannot be met is 'synthetic'—whereas small irrigation works, improved field practices, and more efficient storage, transportation and marketing is 'natural' and acceptable. This predicates the avoidance of mono-agriculture, even at some loss in short term efficiency, in favour of mixed cropping; and particularly suggests the avoidance of mono-agriculture. The expansion of small scale mixed crop agriculture is called for, plus a need to guard against the promotion of large scale agricultural enterprises by state, multinational or private agencies.[16, 17]

Urban areas

Urban places can be defined in quantitative and qualitative terms. Quantitative criteria are useful for enumeration purposes because they facilitate comparability, yet however these kinds of criteria are explained the method of definition is open to challenge on qualitative grounds.[18]

An example drawn from experience in Honduras uses a blend of criteria. Here centres with populations of 1,000 or more are regarded as urban provided they also have:

1 A primary school of six grades, plus

2 A post office or a public telephone or a public telegraph, plus

3 Connection by rail or road with other centres or a regular air or maritime service, plus

4 A piped water service, plus

5 Availability of electricity for lighting.

From the foregoing it can be seen that centres of 1,000 population in the economically more advanced countries would always be regarded as urban, whereas in the poorer countries centres of 5,000 or even 10,000 might well fail to meet the criteria given. Thus, it is expedient to consider centres as urban according to differing criteria in intermediate and poor countries. For intermediate countries the starting range can be considered to be populations from 1,000 to 3,000 provided there exists a range of urban-like facilities such as two trading stores, a postal agency, a primary school, a medical clinic and a road connection to the other centres.[19] In the poor nations the starting range might be populations from 1,000 to 5,000 provided the same qualitative criteria are met. Above all it is not population size that explicitly distinguishes villages from towns, but the level of commercial and social service; thus it is not always useful to adhere to any fixed definition of an urban place according to size of population.

It is in Asia, and to a much lesser extent in West Africa and parts of Central America, that a pattern of urban centres existed before the coming of Europeans. The centres that were created by the colonial powers were firstly settled from coastal trading and missionary stations, and this historical precedent can readily be observed in East Africa, the Malay Archipelago and tropical South America. In all these regions there were very few inland centres. Early European settlement throughout what are now the low income areas was undertaken solely to bolster home industries and to serve capitalist expansion. The tropics provided raw materials in bulk for processing in Europe, and in the course of time tropical people became consumers of manufactured goods. Countries with vast inland regions display similar historical patterns of penetration inland from the most suitable ports to the most profitable resources. A clear perspective for Ghana and Nigeria, both intermediate countries with relatively high road network densities, has been illustrated as an 'ideal-typical sequence of transport development', and an attempt has been made in Diagram 13 to restate and supplement this source.[20] The limits of progress in agriculture are constrained absolutely by the transportation available.

The early colonial period laid an administrative foundation for a long era of relatively slow urban growth.[21] Independence, first in Latin America and later in Africa and Asia, was followed by unprecedented accelerations in urban growth which created the vast new aglomerations which arose in response to the replacement of administrative services supplied from the former colonial power. These may well increase to a much greater extent for, although the actual degree of urbanisation is seldom massive by European and North American criteria, it nevertheless remains true that today in the poorer nations the rate of urbanisation is unprecedented in world history.[22]

Subsistence urbanisation can be classified under two headings, that formed generally by overcrowding the established building stock, and new housing founded in shanty structures. In both the definition of a slum is critical to any official determination of the level of sub-standard living. The solidly constructed *gececonda* of Ankara are generally better than the *favelas, vecindades* and *farriades* of Latin America and the *bidonvilles* of Algeria, and these in turn are better than the *bustoes* of Dacca, whose residents are in turn relatively better off than Bombay's homeless street sleepers.

The use of 'floor space' rather than 'total living space' is an antiquated criterion of measurement of slum living. Diagram 14 relates the rate of room occupancy to the size of dwellings in a way that isolates the countries which are considered to be advanced from a selection of intermediate and poor countries. The information given for low income countries shows a high proportion of small dwellings coupled to a high rate of room occupancy—thus higher national rates of overcrowding.[23] Racial and ethnic heterogeneity, urban migration, a decline in the influence of the extended family and alterations in social responsibilities can all be reflected in slum housing. But by far the most arresting characteristic is the speed with which it has occurred, as echoed in the

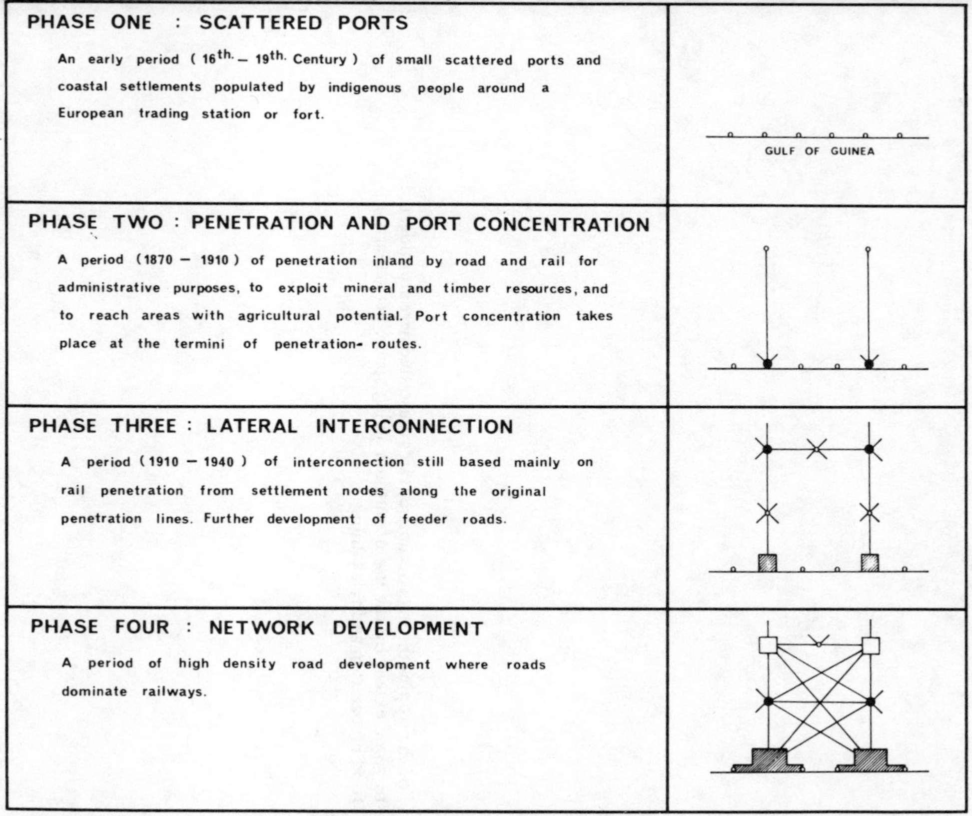

PHASE ONE : SCATTERED PORTS

An early period (16th – 19th. Century) of small scattered ports and coastal settlements populated by indigenous people around a European trading station or fort.

PHASE TWO : PENETRATION AND PORT CONCENTRATION

A period (1870 – 1910) of penetration inland by road and rail for administrative purposes, to exploit mineral and timber resources, and to reach areas with agricultural potential. Port concentration takes place at the termini of penetration- routes.

PHASE THREE : LATERAL INTERCONNECTION

A period (1910 – 1940) of interconnection still based mainly on rail penetration from settlement nodes along the original penetration lines. Further development of feeder roads.

PHASE FOUR : NETWORK DEVELOPMENT

A period of high density road development where roads dominate railways.

GULF OF GUINEA

DIAGRAM 13 EVOLUTION OF LAND BASED TRANSPORTATION IN WEST AFRICA

Data reference: redrawn from Edward J. Jaffe, R.L. Morrill and Peter R. Gould, 'Transport Expansion in Underdeveloped Countries', *The Geographical Review*, vol.LIII, no.4, October 1963.

For the tropics the high occupancy rates illustrated here are mitigated to some extent by the use of outdoor living space, particularly for food preparation and relaxation.

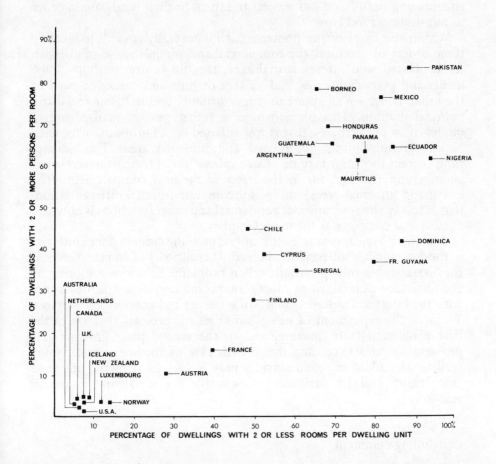

DWELLING SIZE & RATES OF OCCUPANCY FOR SELECTED COUNTRIES

DIAGRAM 14

colourful phrases 'squatter parachutists' and 'mushroom housing'. Changes in the economically threadbare mid 1970s slowed down job availability and the response, already detectable in West Africa, is a reduction in the rural to urban flow of people. The long tail on the queue for urban jobs has the dual effect of discouraging newcomers and encouraging unfulfilled job seekers to return to their rural base in order to put down a food crop.

Within the cities of the poorer areas it is generally possible to identify three orders of precinct: the commercial and administrative centre with its associated well off residential area; the old centre of shops, tenements and petty industries, and an area of huts and shacks on parts of the urban fringe—in all an urban composition bound to foster social and political division. This phenomenon is sometimes rationalised into a model of 'replica' towns; that is towns based on a European image with two geographically distinct 'formal' and 'informal' areas. This assumption, correct though it may be as an explanation of form, is nevertheless an oversimplification; for in the lesser of the neat compartments (the low grade informal areas) there is incomplete internal differentiation; that is to say the separation of residential and other functions is nowhere as clear and complete as the model implies.

A major physical characteristic of fast growing cities in poor countries is the low quality of services. Indeed, the disposal of human faeces is the most stubbornly persistent urban problem. Solutions are beset by the difficulty of reconciling short term production demands for finance with the long term welfare benefits of sewerage and water supply services. To incur the repayment of heavy subsidies for projects that are in the first place non-profit making, and in the second place growing as a problem at rates exceeding the growth rate of income, is clearly unrealistic. In addition, good services play a part in attracting migrants that might well be nationally undesirable for social and economic reasons.

Concluding comment

Because so much emphasis is made of monetary measures it was necessary in this chapter to look further into the factoral basis of underdevelopment. First there is the physical difference between the tropical and temperate environments; for example tropical soils are both more fragile and reactive to severe climatic assaults. A second distinction is culturally based; the Christian ethic generates populations singularly attentive to economic advance, a drive which cannot be as readily identified in low income countries. A third, historical, distinction can be isolated; the dualism induced through colonial administration which separated administrative and entrepreneurial spirit. The consequence of these three main distinctions between the recognisably overdeveloped and underdeveloped lands leads toward an identification of the three main problems in poorer areas today: a movement of people seeking a higher quality of life and the unemployment and urban squalor this consequentially generates; inequalities in income and unfairness in the distribution of education and social goods: and specific failings and inefficiencies in the use of capital.

Fundamentally the plight of the economically disadvantaged in the Southern nations fosters economic privilege and resource capture in the Northern free enterprise and centrally directed nations. This reasoning shows that underdevelopment is linked structurally to overdevelopment. Most low income countries hope to remove these structural ties through trade and excise arrangements and to sustain higher levels of capitalisation coupled to greater output with the help of technological innovation. Negotiated fairly, the prospect of improving the standing of the poorer nations in relation to the more economically advanced nations is reasonable. But UNCTAD and similar negotiations are political gestures dominated by the Northern (particularly transatlantic) nations and designed to secure strategic bases, neutral partners and an assured flow of resources. For this reason, the effectiveness of these negotiations is doubtful, at least from a low income perspective. The gross rate of flow of aid from all sources is undoubtedly increasing, but the *per capita* level of North to South aid is declining, especially for the populous nations; and in terms of financial gearing, the results are very unimpressive. Viewed against the limited flow of official capital for loans and waning private investment, the aggregated local purchasing power is, by the standards of advanced countries, non-competitive and non-strategic. What low income nations might well do as a consequence is to assess their environmental advantages and, taking into account the longer energy outlook, consider an ecodevelopment strategy which guarantees continued, even improved, life support.

Notes

1   William Woodruff, *Impact of Western Man,* St Martin's Press, New York, 1966.

2   Systems analysis is now respectable received wisdom. A useful handbook, edited by John Beishon and Geoff Peters is *Systems Behaviour,* Harper and Row, London, 1976 (second edition).

3   Mumford, a most valued mentor, observed, 'try as we will we cannot grasp more than a fragment of the totality of our living, for to grasp the whole would be to live the whole over again, and that would require another lifetime'. Lewis Mumford, *Findings and Keepings,* Secker and Warburg, London, 1975, p.181.

4   'Black box' is a shorthand expression used by planning theorists to represent a system about which one has an incomplete knowledge excepting the inputs and outputs—internally it is black.

5   Ninety-eight countries with populations in excess of three million are included, with wealthy Kuwait and New Zealand as make-weights for the hundred. In the poor countries the annual GNP *per capita* is less than $200 US per annum; in the intermediate countries the annual GNP *per capita* is between $200 US and the world mean $520 US per annum; and of course in the economically advanced countries the GNP *per capita* is above the world mean. Source: United Nations, Statistical Office, *Statistical Yearbook*(s).

6   Agriculture, forestry, hunting and fishing; (a) extractive industries; (b and c) manufacturing industries; (d) building; (e) electricity, gas water and sanitary services; (f) commerce, insurance and estate management; (g) transport, warehousing and communications; (h) services.

7   K. Marx, *The Economic and Philosophical Manuscripts of 1844,* Progress Publishers, Moscow, 1974, p.145.

8   A useful essay along these lines, 'The Technology of Zero Growth' has been written by Harvey Brooks, in *The No-Growth Society,* American Academy of Science, Autumn 1973.

9   J. Beaujeu-Garnier, translated by S.H. Beaver, *Geography of Population,* Longmans, London, 1966.

10 J.H. Paterson, *Land Work and Resources,* Edward Arnold, London, 1972, p.28.

11 Land rotation and the variants are well described by Clifford Geertz in *Agricultural Innovation: the Processes of Ecological Change in Indonesia,* University of California Press, Berkley, 1971.

12 Fish farming potentials are examined in two *Scientific American* offprints: Clifford B. Pinchot, 'Marine Farming', no.1205, 1970 and S.J. Holt, 'The Food Resources of the Ocean', no.886, 1969.

13 Forest exploitation has been lucidly reviewed by Erik Eckholm in *Losing Ground,* Norton, New York, 1976.

14 Gerald Leach, *Energy and Food Production,* International Institute for Environment and Development, London, 1975.

15 Plant breeders advocate as imperative that the maize, wheat and rice strains now fast going out of use must be stored in genetic grain banks where they can again be brought back into use for re-breeding after widespread total crop failure.

16 The reasoning is only partly political. The only large scaled agri-cultural production schemes that have succeeded are related to

export cropping, and arise in terms of money profits which can never repurchase soil losses. The simple fact of the matter is that natural wastage during the storage, transportation and marketing of an export crop (e.g. cotton in Sudan and tea in Sri Lanka) plus the same list of losses for imported foodstuffs means that food replacement purchases (mainly rice and wheat) are very expensively and inefficiently acquired.

17   The subject of food as aid is examined more fully by Lester R. Brown and Erik P. Eckholm in *By Bread Alone,* Praeger, New York, 1974.

18   Definitions of urban places vary. In China, for example, settlements with over 2,000 inhabitants are accepted as urban whereas the India census sets the lower limit at 5,000 and Japan uses a figure of 30,000. Population studies in a number of African countries have used the somewhat arbitrary population of 5,000 or more as a definition of a town. Reference to European examples is even less helpful, for the base figure is 250 in Denmark, 2,000 in France and 20,000 in the Netherlands.

19   Three thousand plus population would automatically be designated as urban in intermediate countries. Five thousand plus population would automatically be designated as urban in poor countries.

20   Edward J. Taaffe, R.L. Morrill and Peter R. Gould, 'Transport Expansion in Underdeveloped Countries: a Comparative Analysis', *The Geographical Review,* vol.LIII, no.4, October 1963, pp.503-29.

21   Other factors influencing the function and form of settlements include geomorphological, climatic, resources, religious, military, political and socio-cultural desiderata.

22   Urbanisation trends for low income nations are set out by David Turnham and Ingelies Jaeger in Table V10 of *The Employment Problem in Less Developed Countries,* OECD, Paris, 1971.

23   In temperate climates the actual floor space per person accords closely with the total home living space, but in hot climates the home living space may be up to 50 per cent out of doors. Furthermore, the actual floor space required per person is less in low income countries because of the limited range of physical possessions poorer people require to be stored away.

PART II

EXTANT AND ALTERNATIVE DEVELOPMENT SYSTEMS

The next two chapters are concerned, firstly to analyse existing development systems in low income countries (Chapter 4),and then to elaborate upon the alternative ecodevelopment concept (Chapter 5).

4 Development systems in low income countries

The root cause of the (environmental) crisis is not to be found in how men interact with nature, but in how they interact with each other and that to solve the environmental crisis we must solve the problem of poverty, racial injustice and war.

Barry Commoner, 1973[1]

Enough of the factoral basis has been dealt with in the previous chapters to gain an insight into the form, function and dynamics of the man-to-land relationship. The 'black box' within the representation (Diagram 8) depicts the general character of the central development system and the lid on this box can now be lifted and the various contents examined. These are shown in Diagram 15 as the linkages and feedback between values (ideals), external forces (exogenies), and supra-community organisations (policies). This structural arrangement is traced in the passages which follow.

Extant development systems

There has been very little comparative improvement *per capita* economically for the world's poorer nations since Independence. The monetary price paid for their commodities is low and resource depletion is, as a result, too high. It is precisely for these two reasons that political ecology (under other headings) is thrust onto the agenda in negotiations for a new international order—the North-South dialogue.

Nearly all human societies seek consciously to improve their lot through development. In this pursuit they devise 'development systems' at the interface of people with their terrestrial platform. The construct shown holds that within these development systems two powerful organisational forces work upon the ideals of society—namely the exogenous supra-societal influences of international and multinational kinds, and endogenously formed intra-societal policies.

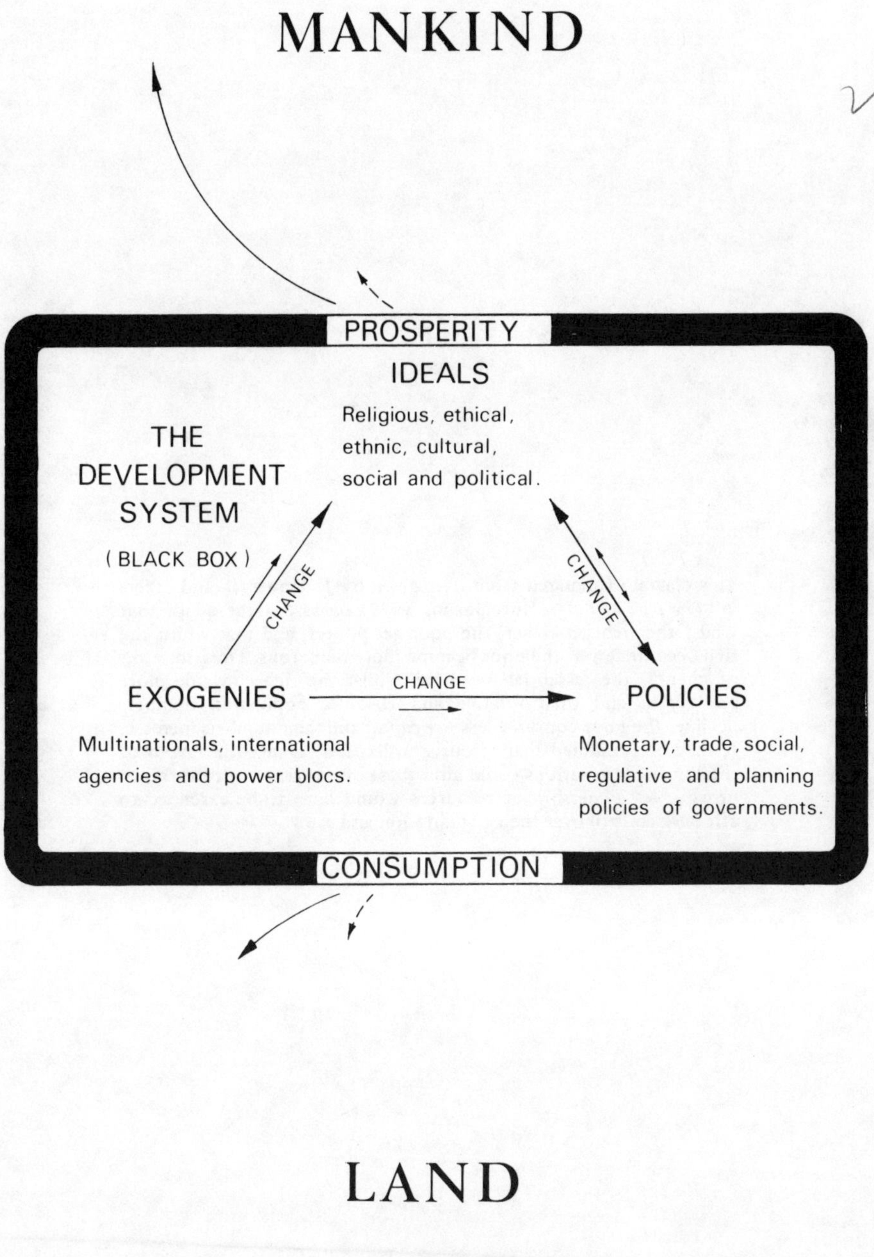

MANKIND

PROSPERITY

IDEALS

Religious, ethical,
ethnic, cultural,
social and political.

THE
DEVELOPMENT
SYSTEM

(BLACK BOX)

CHANGE

CHANGE

EXOGENIES → CHANGE → POLICIES

Multinationals, international
agencies and power blocs.

Monetary, trade, social,
regulative and planning
policies of governments.

CONSUMPTION

LAND

THE DEVELOPMENT SYSTEM

DIAGRAM 15 (inset from Diagram 8)

This diagram (prepared from data given by J. Tinbergen and others in *The RIO Report*, Hutchinson, 1977) bears out the adage that whilst the rich get richer, the poor get poorer; and that whilst the rich become fewer, the poor become more numerous. Thus, in terms of energy, the 'essential' resource, whilst the rich consume more *per capita* and their relative and absolute population numbers decline, the poor consume less *per capita* and their numbers increase. It may be presumed that resource utilisation balanced in favour of the low income nations could alter these dispositions, but for this to prove true, ownership of resources would have to be extended to effective control over their exploitation and sale.

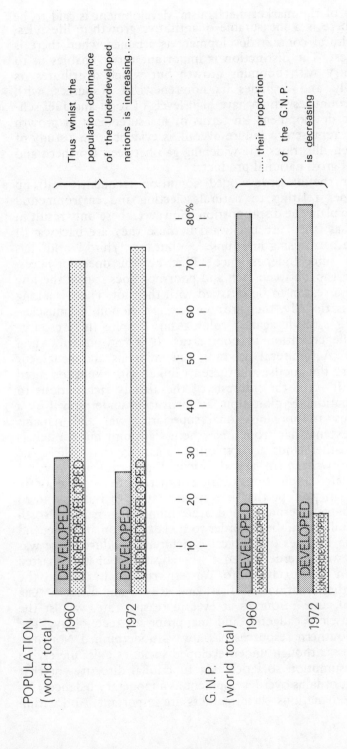

Thus whilst the population dominance of the Underdeveloped nations is increasing....

....their proportion of the G.N.P. is decreasing

POPULATION (world total)

1960

1972

10 20 30 40 50 60 70 80%

G.N.P. (world total)

1960

1972

DEVELOPED
UNDERDEVELOPED

DEVELOPED
UNDERDEVELOPED

DEVELOPED
UNDERDEVELOPED

DEVELOPED
UNDERDEVELOPED

DIAGRAM 16

RELATIVE SHARES OF POPULATION AND G.N.P.

In the context of the market mechanism, development is said to be attained when there is a measurable quantitative growth in lifestyles; whereas in a cultural context development is attained when there is qualitative progress. The distinction is important for it enables us to compare a country with booming growth but which distributes its rewards unequally and degrades its non-renewable resources, with materially poor countries which have high levels of food and fuel self-sufficiency. That development, in terms of measurements of growth can, nevertheless, represent a failure overall, is evident from a study of Diagram 16 which illustrates the widening gap between Northern and Southern levels of gross national product.

Apologists for the underdeveloped condition frequently call up Darwinist analogies relating to natural selection and environmental conditioning to explain the disproportion. However, these only result in tautologies such as 'they are backward because they are backward'! Alternatively, the patronising line runs, '... but the "Third World" has come a long way since Independence'. True, but this does not necessarily narrow the gap between rich and poor nor does it give the low income countries a reason to be satisfied with their lot. There is a long way to go. Organisationally, they are now flexing their political muscle— a heritage of their struggle against colonialism. Despite this, resource exploitation is the condition in poor areas. It is very much a rural focussed activity. Agricultural produce, raw minerals and rough-cut timber characterise the goods: and these are linked with export oriented industrialisation. It is in the interests of the already rich nations to maintain this situation. Exploitation, an institution underpinned by a belief in religious and organisational superiority was and remains parasitic to the extent that from a Northern viewpoint human beings and resources in other lands are exploited to assuage that belief. The consequences are written in the disoriented governments, ravaged resources and sweated populations of the Southern nations. We may fix upon the Hobbesian precept that it is in the nature of humankind to dominate and subjugate resources and other human beings. The North needed minerals, oil and timber in order to fuel expansion at home, and it also desired the luxuries of tropical agricultural produce. Here was the basis of a skewed interdependence whereby the poor areas parted with real wealth in 'fair' exchange for Western trinkets. In this way the transatlantic Northern nations at first, and Russia and Eastern Asia later, grew to consume resources at ever increasing rates; whilst the South received useless gadgetry and inappropriate technology. The degradation of Southern resources has always underpinned Northern profit taking. It is as though underdeveloped societies exist merely to support high consumption societies as a functional directive—or that underdevelopment ordains overdevelopment as a monetary balance.

For the Northern nations their markets are important. And within those markets manpower is more important as a cost consideration than raw materials and waste products. To be organised in this way Northern nations intrude a further environmentally alien component, the urban market place, where labour can be aggregated and regulated. The motives to build cities were seldom sinister; but profit focussed on them and remained immune to the plight of less successful individuals and the depletion of resources. Now the low income nations are standing up to demand a system which gives them fairer terms of trade and which takes away less through the profit stripping of resources. Aid, currently running at less than 1 per cent of GNP in overdeveloped countries, cannot be used to buy a solution to problems of unbalanced production because money as aid is both inefficiently used and creates additional net outflows of profit. The rectification needed in order to attain a position of equity in trading and international dealing is mainly structural.

Ecodevelopment sees monetary equilibrium as only one part of social progress, of which the other components are cultural harmony and ecological balance. In material but non-monetary terms, it might mean:

> . . . organise employment so that all can contribute; to increase productivity in agriculture so that a surplus can be extracted without the need to use brutal methods; to check inequality so as not to waste resources on unnecessary consumption and undermine morale by generating envy; to raise the general level of health and to institute birth control; to build up the basis of heavy industry so as to be able to modernise production as fast as possible, and meanwhile to encourage handicrafts to mechanise themselves by means of 'intermediate techniques'; to spread education and develop self-reliance.[2]

This passage by Professor Robinson derives from the China experience where, admittedly, there have been some miscalculations. Yet the basic policies were correct in their overall stress upon obtaining a balance with the forces of nature, the husbanding of non-replaceable resources, and avoidance of profiteering. It must also be recognised that few countries are as free as China has been from external influences and trading linkages to go it alone. The trappings of colonial allegiance, the inertia caused by cultural dominance and the necessity to trade render it inexpedient at least, foolhardy at most, for other poor countries to accept the China example as copybook. Nevertheless, China does represent a third of the world's population and provides an important case study.

Policy makers with an eye to the Northern development models reason, with false logic, that if pollution results from development then pollution is wanted so that they too can obtain development. This posture, plus a lack of intervention in the forces which lead to population growth and the rapacious exploitation of natural endowments, led former development planners to argue that the proponents of traditional virtues were naively utopian. We have learnt that nations now have to consider the social as well as the economic costs of supplying resources cheaply.[3] Money out must equal, or nearly equal, money in, or there will be runaway fiscal imbalances. The huge volume of unprocessed resources coming from low income areas is nearly balanced, in terms of Northern imputations of monetary worth, by the manufactured goods which flow back to the Southern nations. But the real value of manufactured goods and services in, has never equalled the real value of basic resources out. The reasoning is supported by the enormity (see Diagram 2) of trade internal to the already developed market. This is the monetary representation of what goes on, the manufactured articles being produced, in large measure, from bulk resources obtained cheaply. Thus it can be seen that the market mechanism of the northern, already overdeveloped nations, is a device to get at resources, the real wealth. It has done this on its own terms very efficiently, as Marx had frequently to observe. But now the poor can wield some influence to adjust the mechanism; whilst money in will still, of necessity, equal money out, the future prices put on resources can be adjusted so that real wealth reaps real worth.

From a Marxist standpoint, the main emphasis is not upon natural resources, but concentrates upon the means of production. Socialist analysis is an important consideration for peoples under heavy sub-jugation, but removal of a capitalist yoke for replacement by another elitist hegemony can be painful and pointless. Concern for population numbers, natural resource endowments, socially rewarding work and overall energy and food self-sufficiency are far more important. They are the basis for all sound ecodevelopment irrespective of the political form of organisation. There is hope for separate, probably socialist, policy direction; but in the final event the resource platform on which people live is as important in deciding future policies as politics itself.

It would be a grave error if this sequential account led to the notion that development within any low income country, or indeed the globe itself, can be explained, root, trunk, branch and twig. Development systems are not structured in this way. Two features of studies under-taken at the Massachusetts Institute of Technology, on limits to growth, are of conceptual value, because of the way they emphasise the finite-ness of global resources, and the interconnectedness of human actions.[4] Growing consumer oriented populations will induce environmental change, usually for the worse. Indeed, the only permanent characteristic of the human environment is that it is always changing. The instruments of change are the development system and the power structures. It must be that Southern nations will come to question, then reject, the currently popular development models (capitalist and totalitarian) and see them for what they are—elusive and never fully satisfying. Self-sustaining alternatives will, in turn, be more seriously considered. This will lead to a downturn in Northern profits and, in their terms, monetary disequilibrium; but that for the poorer Southern world is a matter of small account.

Ideals (refer back to Diagram 15)

The ability to act with hindsight and forethought is the distinguishing mark of *homo sapiens,* and caused numerous European philosophers and religious workers in the Middle Ages to set mankind apart from nature as the species ordained to tame the elements and master the environment. With what great success! The notions of natural order as pagan, and Christian dominance as ordained, became set in the post-Hanoverian phoenix of industrialisation and capitalism. Nature could be loved when it was tamed; when it was raw it was to be feared or seen as a challenge. This force can be reckoned as the most powerful in human history. But the imperial prizes sought do not explain the drive to seek them—the motivation. Hungering for creature comforts does not explain the effort consistently made by Northern nations to over-produce and overconsume.

Organised religion, particularly the Protestant and Catholic parts of Christianity, lies at the heart of the lack of conciliation between mankind and nature. There is no denying the pervasive global influence of the Christian ethic upon the environment. Christians will assert that biblical misrepresentations are frequent and unfair, and that the *Old Testament,* in particular, abounds with an understanding of man's dependence on nature. But at the very beginning, *Genesis* 1:28 and 29, and in the more final *Papal Encyclical* of 1967, the subjugation of nature and its command by mankind, indeed a view of nature created, even designed, for mankind, is dominant.[5] Whether wholly attributable to Christian doctrine, or not, the influence upon the environment of Judaic-Christian beliefs, like the relationship between the missionary movement and colonialism, is apparent without necessarily being causal. Christianity has not converted all those without 'the faith', of whatever kind, to its tenets; but quite directly it has induced vast agglomerations to urbanise and fashion anthropocentric attitudes. These, in the main, are the attitudes of leaders in low income countries today; for despite an understanding of natural limits to population and resources, societies are slow to get rid of allegorical beliefs inherited from less well informed times. Indeed, it is easy to plot the geographical expansion of the Christian ethic with capitalist advance. Free enterprise economists have 'confidence' in the bounty of nature to serve consumer needs, and that confidence is backed up by a profound faith in mankind being ordained by God to dominate nature.

The Christian attitude which underlies most development policies in low income areas may be described as cultural determinism. The Christian-cum-colonial doctrine has, somehow, coupled notions of human love to resource ravishment; and has worked well, for a time, in the resource rich, low density lands of the New World; kept the Old World supplied with resources, and created an economic elite in poor countries. Two disastrous consequences are, first, a vast underprivileged class and second, a rapacious run on non-renewable resources.

Despite contemporary understandings of ecology and entropy, mankind is still developing anthropocentrically, in a manner often described as 'human nature after all!' McHarg gives a North American analogy when he states that 'inevitably an anthropocentric society will choose tomato stakes as a higher utility than the priceless and irreplaceable redwoods they have supplanted'.[6] If one set of religious principles has set mankind environmentally adrift, then in this time of effective communication, a new set of refurbished ideals could put mankind to rights. This calls for the revision, re-expression and re-adoption of essentially pantheistic views and values.

Our new understanding of the interworking of natural forces, of human dependence upon finite resources and of the awful arithmetic of population growth, lead us to call for a revised creed which accepts that mankind is not above nature and can only sustain values within nature. Religions of the Orient and the belief of St Francis (the only Christian eco-saint) show the way. A new deity is not the call! It is a call for the recognition of an ideal which works to establish both space and sufficiency for all, now, and for our progeny. If human communities block this ideal, then in many parts of the world they thwart their own survival.

The argument here is that the ideals of individuals and communities is mankind's most powerful commodity. Governments can come and go, as can the supra-national powers, but what matters most are individual beliefs in the worth and continuity of life. An anthropocentric view of the global ecosystems leads, as observed, to a desecration of what is worthy in nature; to uphold what is judged to be worthy in nature shows an acceptance of mankind as part of nature. Although precious to human individuals, these ideals are not environmentally explicit. They embrace abstractions such as virtue, prestige and affection for and from others. It is difficult to define environmental rectitude, but clear away the cluttered thinking that has gone into the formulation of organised religious belief and we see how ideals can be extrapolated into goals for progress without giving up the tenets of religious faith. The conceptual leap does not quite reach the other side, as it were; nevertheless the environmental goals of a non-monetary kind that can be derived, from what are in essence pantheistic ideals, are:

1 Enlarge the capacity of each individual to fulfil his or her

desire to be useful and wanted, thereby dignifying labour intensive and socially directed efforts of environmentally non-violent kinds.

2 Expand the capacity of each community to be self-sufficient, which leads to the regeneration of renewable resources and the careful use of non-renewable resources.

3 Enhance fairness and justice in society which, in environmental terms, means the avoidance of wasteful consumption by any privileged group.

Ideals are essential in all societies, and societies that sacrifice them on ego altars or in market places face moral bankruptcy and environmental degradation. Modern society avoids the embarrassment of consciously educating its young about ideals, thus they now educate themselves. This shift is a recent and popular upswell that has its origins in pantheism and its promotion by means of modern communications.

Exogenies (refer back to Diagram 15)

The fundamental problems of a specifically environmental kind in low income areas are, firstly, to repair the ravages of past exploitation, and secondly, to apply environmentally acceptable policies to development in the future. Yet recognisable environmental failure cannot be explained solely in terms of land using and technical deficiencies. The external influence of dominating pervasiveness was the colonial thrust (based on Christian rectitude) the profit motive and racial elitism. Capitalism is the great persuader. Higher purchasing power and increased varieties of consumer goods leads to more and even more expansion. Aid, in donor terms, is a loss leader; but it binds low income recipients closely to capital growth through resource exploitation rather than human factor needs, such as employment. IMF loan agreements are particularly insistent about exchange and tariff liberalisation, mostly reflected in a freedom to move hard currencies around and to import Western manufactures, yet do not allow workers to migrate freely to seek employment in the rich nations or to export processed materials. This shows a fallacy within such 'liberal' policies, as does the dumping ground mentality of multinational companies wishing to export their pollution problems to countries bound by aid agreements to be receptive to foreign investment. Market economies, left to their own devices, will never opt for no-growth or slow-growth even in the face of dwindling resources. Their problem is one of always having to increase monetary profits—capitalist and much of communism—without profits being a contradiction.

An advanced (Northern) country's public sector has essentially three tasks: to maintain full employment, redistribute income, and provide remedies for market failure. But what is the international analogue? Where is the international deficit spending in the international system? The redistribution of income from rich to poor countries? The remedial policies that offset 'disequalising' market forces, or that correct inappropriate transfers of goods, technology and institutions from the rich countries?[7]

The champions of capitalism and transnationalism would be loath to accept this criticism or to alter course. But arguments favouring adherence to their model must be questioned by the low income nations.[8] The poor Southern majority are humanly suppressed and degraded, and their resources exploited; and there is no way, barring windfall resource finds, by which this aggravation can be reversed.

The multinationals and the development banks are very much a product of, and are in the control of, the Northern transatlantic powers. Centrally directed economies have never exerted influence of the same order, but it would be wrong to anticipate that exploitative and dominating traits do not also emanate from that source. Thus it is the case, especially in relation to resource exploitation, that both the super-blocs of the North (the transatlantic and the centrally directed socialist powers) have proved unreliable. Their common objectives can be traced within international agencies. UNESCO is in Paris. The Food and Agriculture Organisation in Rome, although recently outward looking, has always been a haven for advisors from overdeveloped countries. Only UNEP, the United Nations Environment Programme, is in a low income country, at Nairobi. Yet in these agencies Southern assertiveness, particularly from Africa and the Arabic speaking countries, is working effectively to render the voice of the low income areas audible. Progress is slow; the greatest cash flow via the international agencies is from the money specialist transatlantic nations, and this fact alone causes most people to reflect cynically upon the dent the poorer nations can make in capital intensive policies. The other power blocs are more internally consistent from a low income viewpoint. The cartel blocs, of which OPEC is a forerunner, are important. There is the Arab bloc, the South East Asian financial group, the Colombo group, the Andean Pact and the Third World Nuclear Club. Their motives and their spatial limits often overlap and present a maze of conflicting policies whose only common element, really, is the general absence of environmental considerations!

Policies (refer back to Diagram 15)

Government policies are ground out by the two socio-economic mill-

96

stones examined above; ideals and exogenies. To review policy in terms of central and market economy operations would be to go over ground already covered—but policies of the environmental left and the environmental right are identifiable and should be considered.

The virtues of higher environmental standards are appreciated by both the left and right: but the left and right view the upholding of these standards as benefitting the poor and rich differently. Here is a view from Kapp:

> . . . the growing recognition given in recent years to the phenomenon of social costs reflects merely a shift in the balance of power from those groups in society responsible for initiating economic change to those who bore the brunt of the social losses in the past and who are now using their growing political and economic power in an effort to protect themselves against the undesirable consequences of progress.[9]

Take, as an example, resource conservation; the well-to-do on the Right have no wish to conserve resources they cannot consume themselves (say oil in vast quantities) because the material benefits for them and their progeny now is seen to be 'good' for them. Also 'good' for them is the preservation of places of beauty and recreation, as they alone can afford the cost of transport. The Left, on the other hand, would want (in our case of oil) to nationalise production, restrict exports and use this energy for everybody, particularly to power construction and to manufacture fertilisers. Left and Right also differ in their approaches to environmental protection. One feature in common is that both want a clean environment, but the Right strive generally to attain this by making the consumer pay a regressive clean-up tax; whereas the Left adopts a polluter-pays reasoning. These two examples illustrate the internal political dilemma imposed by political allegiance.

Another source of confusion in policy formulation arises from what Mahbub ul Haq describes as 'development fashions'.[10] He observes two 'about turns' for Pakistan since independence; import substitution to export expansion and industrialisation to agriculture. He also notes two abrupt changes in direction, on population and income distribution. The environmental component associated with changes of these kinds can only be partially explained in terms of policy differences between left and right. The real reason for environmental inconsistency is that the environmental dimension seldom struck policy planners as important enough to be taken into account. For them monetary consistency was more significant; it mattered not whether a plan was resource depleting or environmentally damaging, so long as the trading books could be either balanced or systematically explained away. If political directives came from the right the necessary objective was to raise the marginal return on capital investment relative to labour, thereby favouring industry and a Green Revolution; whereas with political directives from the Left lower marginal returns would be acceptable from higher labour input (particularly in small scale industry and agriculture) as being consistent with a policy of lower capitalisation.

In democracies, when one party is in, a civil service interprets policy their way; when an alternative party is in then policy is reinterpreted accordingly. In the more usually encountered singularly directed economies, both Left and Right, the political line translates into civil service rubric. Right wing political dominance frequently produces environmental preservation policies that would warm the heart of the most tentative environmentalists, whereas Left wing dominance will be concerned to establish an ideological toehold even if the environmental price that has to be paid is high. This argument can, of course, be turned the other way around.

What is of environmental interest is the element of pantheistic content in government policy; Papua New Guinea is to the fore here and the government has enshrined self-sufficiency beliefs in development policies. Some larger countries, notably China, Burma and Tanzania, have made similar moves. Policies for self-reliance are not easy to enforce because of the hindrance presented by the existing nodes and networks of government. Their distribution systems, from colonial times, were predominantly concerned with order; whereas the new distributive system is concerned with equity. The new movement therefore derives its effectiveness not so much from administrative integrity as from moral conviction. It represents a renewal of indigenous discipline temporarily fallow during periods of colonial intervention. New eco-development policies would:

1 Keep paper money and real resources in true wealth perspective.

2 Ensure that trade policies are consistent with real needs.

3 Pass and enforce statutes which ensure an equitable distribution of the benefits of development in a way which abates pollution and which gives equal access to recreation environments.

4 Advance planning policies which ensure that natural resources, recreational assets and environmental quality are treated as the most important elements of local and regional plans.

Such policies for low income areas are against unequal advantage, and for fair distribution. There is little room here for the civil service pragmatism so often represented by plans for a technological fix, selling to the highest bidder, or multinational agreements. It thus appears that environmentally consistent internal policies could become the hallmark of progressive development in the poorer Southern nations.

Modelling the environmental component in development systems

In the opening section of this chapter the causes and effects of extant development systems were critically reviewed. We must be careful about tampering with ecological systems of any kind, simply because of the unpredictable consequences which may follow; the North—South global model has, however, to be 'tampered' with because of the human unfairness it perpetrates. A new form of 'new deal' is required. Its major concerns are to overcome poverty, inequality, unemployment, disease and malnutrition. The relationship between population, resources and technology in the new model must be understood in order to appreciate which mix of these variables is the best to adopt in different contexts. The problem is mainly one of understanding where the knowledge we have can be applied with greater wisdom in the future.

Put simply, there are two parts to the human environment. One comprises the God given natural spaces and resources; the other includes man made adaptations. We can add to this model by acknowledging the attachment of human beings to values and beliefs (extrinsic resources) and treat this as an extra ingredient. Structurally the human environment, together with these values and beliefs, can be shown thus:

The human ecosystem Σ

- Human ideals (religious and cultural, values and beliefs)
- Natural spaces (flora, fauna, water and minerals)
- Adapted spaces (building stock and communication channels)
- Human activities (work, play, education)

Tracing the interaction between these components is both difficult and unproductive because the model is not assertive enough to establish where the key controls are. The only certain consequence is a compounding of confusion, although more can perhaps be expected of such modelling endeavours as cybernetics advance.

One modelling device is the replication of human ecosystems in graphic models. In the more direct forms the components are boxed up and labelled.[11] Progressing from this there is the two dimensional 'environmental pie' of Dansereau, and the three dimensional 'biology layer cake' of Odum.[12] All futile effort: human ecology is, after all, more variagated. This realisation comes home when one attempts a graphic identification of the functions and interests involved in a single project. The following structural representation in Diagram 17, complicated although it may appear, leaves one to assume natural spaces and adapted spaces exist merely to accommodate the project. Social goals are, as such, omitted!

A more sophisticated attempt at the formulation of environmental equations introduces an interesting dynamism absent in graphic models. These are all characterised by the fact that 'environmental degradation is not the sum of independent causes, it is the multiplicative product of interconnected ones'.[13] These are the words of the Ehrlichs and Holdren. A re-expression of their equation runs:

Environmental degradation (D) = Population (P)

        × Consumption of goods per person (C)

        × Environmental impact per unit of consumer goods per person (I)

Thus (D)   = P × C × I

In fact, as multiplication is merely addition writ large, twice the population, or consumption, usually more than doubles environmental degradation. What these authors probably had in mind was to express an exponential factor for one or other of the elements (P, C or I) in their equation. Another expression, described as neo-Malthusian, runs:

Standard of living (S)   = Resources (R)

        × Technology (T)

        + Population (P)

$$\text{Thus } S = \frac{R \times T}{P}$$

As R for most low income purposes has to be considered finite, it is only by the increase of technology and the decrease of population that the standard of living can be raised and pollution decreased. Both equations have a common factor, population (P); but

$$P = \frac{D}{C \times I}$$

in the Ehrlich expression compares equally meaninglessly with

$$P = \frac{R \times T}{S}$$

in the neo-Malthusian expression.[14]

The synergistic inputs to any model are clearly more important than the logistic inputs. A paper by Commoner, Corr and Stamler (understandably concerned more with Northern pollution than resource degradation in Southern regions) arrives at an interesting conclusion:

> The predominant factor in our industrial society's increased environmental degradation is neither population nor affluence, but the increasing environmental impact per unit of production due to technological changes.[15]

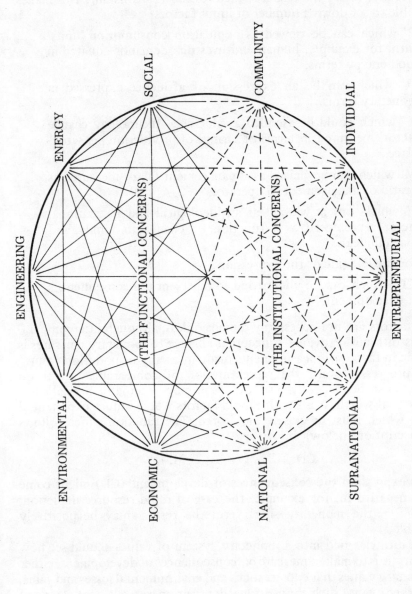

PROJECT LINKS AND INTERESTS

DIAGRAM 17

SOCIAL

COMMUNITY

ENERGY

INDIVIDUAL

ENGINEERING

(THE FUNCTIONAL CONCERNS)

(THE INSTITUTIONAL CONCERNS)

ENTREPRENEURIAL

ENVIRONMENTAL

SUPRANATIONAL

ECONOMIC

NATIONAL

Not everybody would be happy about the appearance of 'affluence' in this quote but the general stress on technology in the form of industry, factory farming and non-degradable waste disposal would generally find adherents in overdeveloped as well as underdeveloped countries.

What is useful in any particular case of environmental assessment is, conceptually, to set the resource factor aside as a constant. This makes it possible to set down a number of input factors:

'P' which can be viewed as population consumption 'units' with, for example, human and livestock demands equated in food energy terms.

'A' which can be an expression of affluence expressed in monetary terms.

'T' which could be ascribed a value as a 'technology change factor' measured in terms of change of production per workplace.

'M' which can be viewed as a management factor measured as a ratio of management to operators.

'I' which can be viewed as an ideological and institutional factor represented as a function of change in family and societal ideals.

And, for the left side of the expression:

'CD' which can be understood to represent the consequences of development.

These factors are not necessarily dimensionless, although intercomparability is difficult. Provided conceptual alliance to monetary measures is set aside in favour of measurements made in energy or pollution equivalents, progress toward the representation of comparable effects on resources can be made. Even so, the result may be a mathematical maze of little real worth. It is the threshold factors which induce exponential change which must be closely monitored. The function which follows (with ascriptions below) shows this.

$$CD \quad \Sigma \quad f\,(P, A, T, M, I)$$

In this expression the consequences of development (CD) might come out as negative in, for example, the case of rapid resource depletion, although in the monetary short term the results may be positively profitable.

Bureaucracies tied into a monetary system of values should see how necessary it is to make a measure of 'consequences of development' either in monetary values that express social and environmental losses and gains, or in other quanta such as nutritional deprivation, resettlement costs and human misery. Thus, more fully, in regard to the above equation:

'P' (population measured in terms of consumption units) has quite absolute effects. A doubling of human numbers in Brazil could be accommodated with environmental consequences that need not be serious; but a doubling of population in the Philippines is unthinkable.

'A' and 'T' (affluence and technology) are put together, but are not multiplied. Technology always relates to affluence, but in varying degree because of the varying environmental consequences arising from technology. Thus enormous increases in Saudi Arabian affluence went more to purchase consumer durables rather than infrastructure and industry thereby registering as a relatively insignificant environmental impact. In contrast, bore hole irrigation in Pakistan has induced a relatively major and favourable environmental impact from a low incidence of cost.

'M' (the management factor) is essentially non-quantifiable, yet the consequences of an environmental kind are readily apparent. Consider Burma and Brazil. In Burma localisation can be criticised in terms of low production, but the strictly environmental consequences of such local management are minimal; whereas in Brazil the admission of exogenous management (e.g. the Volkswagen company and the Ludwig empire in Amazonia) has resulted in catastrophic, almost instantaneous, environmental change. Management motive is an environmentally significant force.

'I' (the ideological and institutional factor) is, like management, difficult to quantify in itself, although the environmental consequences of ideological and institutional shifts can be great. Two contrasting examples from Kenya and China serve to make the point. In Kenya, against all advice, a charcoal export trade was permitted which exploited trees in the coastal hill regions with considerable environmental damage; in China we see the opposite in the reafforestation of formerly denuded hillsides.

The numerical ascription to CD is irrelevant; what is important in any particular case is the causative shift in any one or a combination of factors which induce environmental change. Consider, as a hypothetical example, a doubling of the Argentinian population, involving a doubling of their meat consumption inducing other proportional change in that particular environment. Similar population and consumption changes in Indonesia would induce environmental collapse. Likewise, a mining activity can destroy an environment yet, as is often the case, a relatively small investment in abatement technology can result in a dramatic lowering of environmental impact. It is by looking to the equation as an indication of thresholds that an assessment can be made of environmental 'goods' foregone by technological consumption, and managerial 'bads' creating environmental degradation. In effect the expression is an alternative to assessments of development impact in monetary terms. When populations burgeon, consumption rockets, non-degradable wastes pile up and something has to give; it cannot always be the environment because its absorptive capacity is limited.

New directions

This chapter has been concerned with presenting a critique of development systems, yet in a general way it has led to a preliminary expression of alternatives to contemplate. One is what Brookfield describes as 'a new understanding of man(kinds) changing use of environment and his relationship to the environment'.[16] Here this 'understanding' is expressed in terms of individual, community and societal concepts equating respectively with usefulness, self-sufficiency and fairness. The reintroduction of indigenous ideals over imported procedures is perhaps the most powerful tool in the lockers of low income nations.

> The starting-point for talking about development is our vision of what society should be like: how men and women should live and how they should get along, how groups can co-exist, how the values of our society can be maintained and enhanced. Most of us already have a good idea of the kind of values and the kind of society we want to build. We want to preserve our traditional family ties. We want to preserve the sense of group solidarity that exists in most of our societies. We want to preserve people's attachment to their land. We want improvement in the living standards of people, so that no one need go hungry, and no one need lack medical care, for example. We want the chance to improve ourselves, to learn new ways of doing things—but within the framework of our traditional values.[17]

In that statement socio-environmental goals are explicit; and the subservience of monetary growth policies is implicit. This philosophy lies at the heart of ecodevelopment.

Notes

1 Barry Commoner, *Ecology and Social Action,* University of California Press, Berkeley, 1973.

2   Joan Robinson, *Freedom and Necessity*, Allen and Unwin, London, 1970.

3   Social cost (also described occasionally as diseconomies or negative externalities) indicate community burdens such as the cost of public health or private vehicle smog. Social costs are a negative form of economic externalities.

4   Donella H. Meadows, Dennis L. Meadows, et al., *The Limits to Growth*, Earth Island, London, 1972; and Jay W. Forrester, *World Dynamics*, Wright-Allen, Massachusetts, 1971.

5   *Genesis:* 'The Lord God gave man dominion over the fish in the sea and the fowl in the air, and over every living being that moves upon the earth'. The 1967 Papal Encyclical was titled 'The Development of Peoples' and restated the notion in *Genesis* that the earth was created by God for the use and enjoyment of man.

6   Ian L. McHarg, *Design with Nature*, Doubleday, New York, 1971, p.26.

7   Gerald M. Meier, *Problems of Cooperation for Development*, Oxford University Press, New York, 1974, p.16.

8   However, Northern based writers such as E.J. Mishan in *The Costs of Economic Growth* and J.K. Galbraith in *The Affluent Society*, are far from euphoric about capitalist achievement.

9   K.W. Kapp, *The Social Costs of Private Enterprise*, Schocken Books, New York, 1971, p.16.

10 Mahbub ul Haq, *The Poverty Curtain*, Columbia University Press, New York, 1976.

11 An example is given as 'The Man—Nature System' by C. Chadwick, *Systems View of Planning*, Pergamon, London, 1971.

12 Pierre Dansereau, 'The Human Predicament' in *Human Ecology*, Proceedings of the First Commonwealth Conference on Development and Human Ecology, Charles Knight, London, 1972; also Eugene P. Odum, *Fundamentals of Ecology*, Saunders, Philadelphia, 1971, p.4.

13 P.R. Ehrlich, A.H. Ehrlich and J.R. Holdren, *Human Ecology*, Freeman, San Francisco, 1973, p.12.

14 Population, a factor common to all equations can produce environmental effects that are in inverse proportion. For example, high animal protein consumers, and populations where livestock are venerated, obviously affects the 'P' factor massively; and at higher population densities thresholds can work synergistically to induce grassland exhaustion and soil salination.

15   Barry Commoner, Michael Corr and Paul Stamler, 'The Causes of Pollution', *Environment,* vol.13, no.3, April 1971.

16   Harold Brookfield, *Interdependent Development,* Methuen, London, 1975, p.209.

17   J. Momis, 'Taming the Dragon', edited by Peter Sack, in *Problems of Choice,* National University Press, Canberra, 1974.

5 Life support guidelines

> Force is a physical power. I do not see how its
> effects could produce morality. To yield to force is
> an act of necessity, not of will; it is at best an act
> of prudence. In what sense can it be a moral duty?
>
> *Jean-Jacques Rousseau* 1772[1]

We have seen how purposefully both centrally directed and free enterprise endeavours operate to consume the non-renewable resources of low income areas: this is the unacceptable role of Northern overdevelopment.[2] Faltering corrective steps are being taken by Papua New Guinea, Sri Lanka, Cuba and Zambia to appraise and discuss the human consequences of planned development; and more positive strides have already been taken by China, Burma and Tanzania (in all about half the 'Third World' population) to move toward a self-reliant relationship between population, resources and material wellbeing. These are now examples of ethical planning—in a word, ecodevelopment. Here the Southern nations have had one considerable advantage in that they are accessories to, rather than the originators of, ecological problems.

This means that the poor can draw on the sad experience of Northern nations. A less obvious historical advantage is that the Southern nations have the experience of colonialism to motivate them to look behind the ecodevelopment model to ensure that this is not exploitation and dominance in a new guise.

A hundred years ago the doomwatchers were heralding the end of the world; today the situation, with four times the population, is seen in much the same terms![3] This fatalistic introspection of mankind, which seems almost to will a break in genetic continuity, has to be tempered with an optimism about future survival. Provided global nuclear warfare is averted, the world remains a long way short of environmental collapse, even though it is a vastly changed world. In fact, there are two main environmental problems. One is to forestall the population living on a finite terrestrial platform from crossing the threshold where reasonable material comfort and nutrition can no longer be sustained; and the other is to resist the irreversible environmental damage created by the use of inappropriate technologies.

Development problems are similarly of two main kinds. The first, pollution, is a consequence of inappropriate technological innovation and the solution called for is development control which obviates waste generation. The second, more serious, development problem is that of adjusting to an improved middle way between resource profligacy for a few and poverty for the masses. The main objective for all nations is survival first followed by an improvement upon existing poverty conditions and this, in essence, is the integral component within the eco-development philosophy.

Free enterprise systems cannot readily achieve this objective in low income nations: planning for collective needs through the interruption of market forces and the active promotion of the equitable distribution of production is necessary. One significant environmental advantage with a policy for equity in distribution is that it controls resource utilisation to agreed levels; and if this is still materially inadequate, to seek other ways, such as population limitation, to increase the resource supply. In this way redistribution based on equity conserves resources and enables levels of pollution to be more easily agreed. Steady state policies which seek to arrive at an equilibrium of population size, resource consumption and pollution emission are more realistic and representative of mature 'development' than growth proposals.

The font is always political but the drive has largely to come from the administrative service. This is particularly the case in regional planning, as a custodian of resources. Here, at the heart of the political-administrative alliance called into being to achieve material and social advance, a sound grasp of the logic of ecodevelopment and of the values on which it is based, are essential to policy implementation.

The ecodevelopment philosophy

Ecodevelopment is growth development with a progressive component of environmental concern. It is undoubtedly 'appropriate' development. But to claim that it must accord with environmental rectitude is vacuous. Nevertheless, it remains as difficult to apply *pareto dicta* to ecodevelopment as it is to what Reder described in 1947 as the new standard definition of welfare 'increasing whenever one or more individuals become more satisfied without any other individuals becoming less satisfied'.[4] Ecodevelopment can be likened to the notion of thresholds beyond which more options are closed than are opened as there is further growth in consumption. Helpful though this is to understanding, it does little to map out the way to proceed, because of the inherent difficulties in defining, evaluating and comparing the benefits and losses involved. Perhaps this explains some of the inconsistency in past prescriptions of welfare policy. Ward and Dubos noted for the benefit of the Stockholm environmental conference in 1972 that policy makers can oscillate right across the Christian-pantheist spectrum:

- some are more impressed by the stability and resiliance of ecosystems than by their fragility.

- some would emphasise human settlements rather than natural ecosystems and nature conservation.

- some would give priority to water pollution, others to the state of the atmosphere, still others to the problems of land management.

- some believe that environmental pollution and the depletion of natural resources can best be controlled by individual behaviour, others by a complete transformation of the political structure of lifestyles.

- some believe that the most destructive forms of ecological damage flow from types of high energy high profit technology whose advantages are grossly overstated in terms of genuine utility, others see energy as the key to the basic economic achievement of producing more goods for fewer inputs and thus incomparably widening the citizen's wealth and choice.

- some see the solution of environmental problems in more scientific knowledge and better technological fixes, others in socio-economic morality, and still others in the cultivation of spiritual values.[5]

To an extent these oscillations are acceptable, reflecting the different development systems at work in the urban—industrial and rural—agricultural policy sectors. Consider the following antinomies which are an intentional caricature of rural and urban living:

Rural	Urban
Past	Future
Natural	Cultural
Agrarian	Industrial
Rustic	Technological
Empirical	Theoretical
Noble	Corrupt
Homogenous	Heterogenous

Mindful of these, we can return to the main finding of the previous chapter and contemplate, afresh, the three 'ideals' lit upon:

1 Enlarge the capacity of individuals to fulfil the desire to be useful and wanted, thereby dignifying labour intensive and socially directed efforts of environmentally non-degrading kinds.

2 Expand the capacity of communities to be self-sufficient thereby leading to the replenishment of renewable resources, and the careful use of non-renewable resources.

3 Enhance the fairness and justice of society thereby, in environmental terms, avoiding wasteful consumption by any section or class.

Aligning the ecodevelopment concept with these ideals bring welfare criteria into practical consideration. Answers are now suggested to the question 'what and why'? whilst a project is under consideration, and 'how and when'? whilst it is being implemented. Furthermore, these three ideals allow us to form an accommodation between urban and rural lifestyles.

It is in the urban areas where the basis of life (clean air, fresh water, suitable clothing, nutritious food and appropriate shelter) are most often denied the masses whilst the self-serving minorities go on capturing and enjoying abundance. Social justice is a matter of also ensuring a right of access by all human beings to healthy habitats, and a recognition that a denial of this right through the workings of protection or privilege is an injustice. This means that problems arise from modes of production which cannot be solved by searching for technological alternations. Control over rather than ownership of production is important. It is also a policy of optimism, founded on ecodevelopment's double trinity—economic, social and environmental wellbeing for individuals, communities and society. Nation by nation this form of determinism will produce different consequences. But within nations equality of wealth and income (or at least the avoidance of extremes of poverty and excesses of wealth) will greatly strengthen ecodevelopment policy. This is so because ecodevelopment abstracts the wasteful, competitive

110

resource-capture mentality from development, and aims to free even the most insecure from uncertainty of access to a healthy habitat and the fulfilment of basic needs.

Ecodevelopment principles

The previous statements are intended to form a reconciliation between economic values and ecological virtues. Improving the quality and variety of life is a common goal—achieved through the distribution of increased purchasing power earned from conventional development coupled to the provision of a healthy habitat through environmental management. The latter implies a concept of stewardship wherein mankind has a duty, beyond immediate interests, of establishing societal responsibilities within national ecosystems. The priority for this generation is to limit populations and husband resources whilst avoiding mechanistic alliances to dogma espoused for its political principle rather than its ecodevelopment content. Production solely for the purpose of political control will always be justified by individuals. By contrast, ecodevelopment is powered by societal progress rather than individual gain or glory. Yet it cannot be overlooked that the most important component in society is the individual, and one by one what individuals want is an improved variety and quality to life, formerly 'sought' through development and now capable of being 'attained' through ecodevelopment.

Ecodevelopment is not simply a matter of choosing between socially desirable and extractive policies. It is a combination of, and an equilibrium between, both. But for low income areas, the dilemma runs deeper in two ways. Firstly, in any truly poor nation when there is a proposal for the conservation of resources for the future it has to be agreed that present needs win over environmental protection—or people before conservation. Secondly, in all cases where there are proposals for an expansion of production, care has to be taken to assess whether or not this could result in an overall reduction in the quality of life through, for example, pollution and dumping. It has been observed that, 'growth is not always in the interest of present people and conservation is not always in the interest of future people'[6] thereby re-emphasising the fact that the broadly social and specifically political support given to ecodevelopment is as important as its economic and technological components.

The split between a resource dependent technological state pursuing economic growth and a resource balancing sufficient state seeking human progress can be calibrated, somewhat notionally, as follows:[7]

Technological state	Sufficient state
Resource capturing	Resource sufficient
Accumulates waste	No ultimate wastes
Industrial and urban	Agricultural and rural
Socially fragmented	Socially cohesive
Mankind against nature	Mankind with nature
Pursuing profit	Seeking satisfaction
Large underemployment	Full employment
Internationally focussed	Internally focussed
Capital intensive	Labour intensive
Incomprehensible	Comprehensible
Quantitative	Qualitative
Optimising	Satisfying

Those who desire immediate gratification would opt for the techno-logical state on the ground that individual consumption now is worth more than consumption later by persons as yet unknown and unborn. It therefore becomes a role for political and administrative agents in human communities to consider which goals of society are above individual consumer interests, and to work toward that politically determined collective condition, the sufficient (or self-reliant) state. Such a state must be ecologically healthy; and it must work for the interests of the whole community and for the life period of the youngest members. To this extent the sufficient state is normative, but tending toward the probabilistic in that it leads on to an improved, if not vastly altered, future.

The policy decisions inherent in opting for a sufficient state are clear item by item in the technological versus sufficient tabulation; the goals being determined by the balance struck, in each case, *between:*

1 Economic independence and economic wellbeing (which also raises the important matter of the distribution of goods).

2 High and low variety in human fulfilment.

3 Social justice and individual liberty.

4 Setting social aims and production goals.

5 Uses of resource capital and human labour.

6 Autarchy and foreign trade.

7 Now and the future.

From these fundamental decisions other more specific policy guidelines of an economically fair, environmentally balanced and socially just form can be derived.

112

Ecodevelopment desiderata

Environmental management is hackneyed. Social and economic policy labelled 'ecodevelopment' infers the elaboration of harmony between the natural and social sciences. Within this it is difficult, and rather pointless, to identify the specifically environmental parts. In the main, ecodevelopment policy is concerned with growth and progress set in a context of resource conservation and environmental protection. The eradication of poverty, the elimination of disease, the provision of socially gainful employment, the pursuit of self-reliance and the other principles detailed in Chapter 1 are also central to an understanding of ecodevelopment. Few of these items are specifically environmental. The main desiderata are as follows:

Guideline 1: With the exception of the 'big proposal' (see Chapter 9) ecodevelopment works best from the bottom up. Of course such matters as defence, foreign policy and law and order are issues necessitating decisions of a central kind. But in respect of ecodevelopment, the main centralised matters are directives from information ministries about levels of capitalisation, skills of personnel and propriety of technologies. Ecodevelopment works best, primarily, as a grass roots endeavour.

Guideline 2: As the most effective operational base for ecodevelopment is local and regional, its incorporation into subnational government and planning processes (regional, rural and urban) usefully enables it to grow on the local foundations for government that have already been laid.

Guideline 3: Guideline 2 does not mean that ecodevelopment favours second rate organisation or makeshift reforms when a total restructuring or overhaul is indicated.

Guideline 4: A central question is one of distribution: a first step being to stop waste in order to make gains against basic poverty. Proposals designed to eradicate basic poverty and achieve widespread employment must have the highest priority. This means that any proposal inducing a change in consumption which cannot be traced to direct improvements in the distribution of goods should be postponed. Thus the Northern concept of monetary expansion as a general good has to be replaced with a Southern insistence on policies showing specific benefits.

Guideline 5: The self-reliant component within ecodevelopment policy supposes the use of locally available resources (even when this policy is marginally non-competitive) and,

113

conversely, is against the use, as far as possible, of foreign assistance and technology.

Guideline 6: Ecodevelopment requires that all common property resources (air, water, sub-surface minerals) be constituted in public ownership.

Guideline 7: The consequences of ecodevelopment must be explained in monetary and resource (particularly energy) terms as profits, losses and externalities.

Guideline 8: The polluter-pays-principle must be operated by defining acceptable pollution standards as variously determined from nation to nation and region to region within nations.

Guideline 9: The pursuit of ecodevelopment policies will be much facilitated by focussing upon methods of control and the means of production rather than the actual ownership of resources.

These straightforward guidelines are against foreign capital assistance on the ground that this is more usually an avenue which leads to the exploitative manipulation of the resources, labour and environments of low income recipients. Far from thwarting consumption, the more efficient use of resources, generation of local employment, avoidance of pollution and waste dumping and the attainment of environmental equilibrium, culminates in an overall enhancement of material standards of living. Observance of the foregoing policy guidelines for ecodevelopment ensures, in a practical way, that the level of foreign investment, the scale of projects, and policies for local self-reliance are linked effectively and directly to implementation.

There are three important sub-sets to ecodevelopment policy: Chapter 6 deals with resources and the population mix, Chapter 7 with the relationship of ecodevelopment to economics and Chapter 8 with the balance between appropriate technology and self-reliance.

Notes

1   Jean-Jacques Rousseau, *The Social Contract,* 1772.

2   Underdevelopment implies a conscious, probably colonial, denial, obstruction or misdirection of development. A condition which might be described as 'underdevelopment' or 'predevelopment' can also be identified in sparsely settled landscapes as a form of frontier underdevelopment.

3   D.H. Meadows, D.L. Meadows, et al., *The Limits to Growth*, Earth Island, London, 1972.

4   M.W. Reder, *Studies in the Theory of Welfare Economics*, Columbia University Press, New York, 1947, p.14.

5   Barbara Ward and René Dubos, *Only One Earth*, Penguin Books (Andre Deutsch), London, p.27.

6   Hugh Stretton, *Capitalism Socialism and the Environment*, Cambridge University Press, Cambridge, 1976, p.4.

7   Restated from David Dickson's *Alternative Technology*, Fontana/Collins, Glasgow, 1974, p.103.

PART III
STRATEGIES

This section of the book ends with an expression of operational tactics (Chapter 9) preceded by Chapters 6, 7 and 8 which review, in some detail, the strategies deriving from ecodevelopment concepts.

6 Resources and population

> From the cradle to the grave everyone is dependent
> on nature for an absolutely continuous supply of
> energy in one or other of its numerous forms. When
> the supplies are ample there is prosperity, expansion
> and development. When they are not, there is want.
>
> *Frederick Stoddy,* 1912[1]

It is now necessary to look at the way population expansion works in
relation to the use of resources and to see what relevant conclusions
may be drawn. The present pattern of this relationship, and its consequences for the future, may be simply expressed like this:

$$\frac{\text{ever depleting non-renewable resources}}{\text{ever expanding population}} = \begin{array}{l}\text{increasing} \\ \text{austerity}\end{array}$$

As yet there is no sign that this process is changing. This prompts the
question 'what would happen were popular growth models able to heap
greater amounts of consumer goods onto more people from a dwindling
larder?' Also, there is the dismal population corollary to consider: that
reverse spiral in the poor areas where, despite genuflections to growth,
increasing populations face resource degradation and utter austerity,
achieving consciously through human agency what other ecosystems
would never do, namely growing to a state of overpopulation. The fact
is that resources, particularly fossil fuel energy resources, simply do not
exist in sufficient quantity to supply protein rich diets and put self-
propelled wheels under the world's population now, or ever. Solutions

119

The 'goods' shown are labelled as consumer durables, but GNP would have served our purpose equally well. With 'bads' it is another matter. The 'bad' shown here is pollution; other 'bads' include aesthetic degradation and social diseases. Both consumer durables and pollution are capable of crude monetary measurement. More specifically, as a nation climbs out along the curve there are direct economies ('goods') and diseconomies ('bads') that can be measured; but equally important today are those public welfare 'goods' and social cost 'bads' that fall outside 'free seller—willing buyer' market transactions. They are, by nature, difficult to price in money terms.

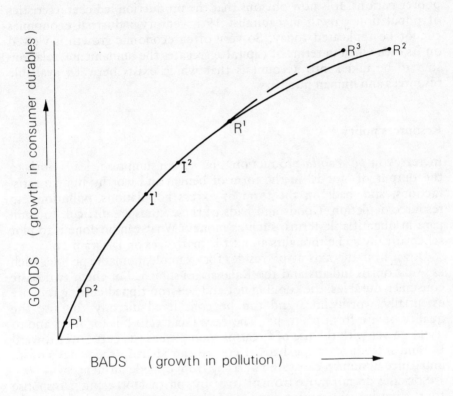

GOODS & BADS I

DIAGRAM 18

121

to the basic problems created by burgeoning populations and dwindling resources were identified in Chapter 3 as twofold: to limit future population and to attain a materially self-sufficing existence for those now living. Both solutions are frustrated by practical constraints: the ethical resistances which ensure that to some extent couples plan their families without regard to the population policies of their countries; and the quantitative finiteness of resources.

Population increase has usually outstripped economic growth in the poorer nations. It is now obvious that the production led characteristics of population growth in capitalist 19th century industrial economies cannot be replicated today. So very often economic growth is viewed on its own when in terms of capital aggregates the fundamental relationship to be taken into account is that which exists between available resources and human numbers.

Resources policy

Increases in *per capita* production, and so consumption, leads both to the output of 'goods' in the form of benign and worthy human satisfactions, and 'bads' in the form of excess populations, pollution and resource depletion. Goods and bads of these kinds are difficult to compare in quantifiable terms, such as money. What can be done is to plot schematically some thoughts about the matter, as on Diagram 18.

Down near the axis at p^1 reside, for example, nomadic peoples such as Amazonian Indians and the Kalahari Bushmen. For them two basic consumer durables, the cooking pot and the iron tipped cutting tool are essentially worthwhile, and can be considered directly to raise the quality of life from p^1 to p^2. The easy facility to kill for food and to wield power with the use of firearms soon pushes the curve over toward I^1, and introduces some bads. Here we can identify the genesis of an imbalance in human ecosystems arising from outside influences.

Societies do not move from p^1 to p^2 by spiritual force, but in response to a stimulus for consumerism or a desire to exert control over the circumstances of their own lives. In itself this can hardly be faulted, for life without these basic consumer durables is an elemental combat. Amazonian Indians slay the turtles needed for food and the jaguars required for garments and cordage in order to acquire some relatively inessential 'trade' trappings. This is understandable; but not much further along the curve, less essential articles such as missionary dresses will be in demand, followed closely by cassette recorders and wristwatches and the first induced 'bad' of a social kind—of which the most notorious is introduced disease. The point is that for low subsistence people, moving to subsistence-plus levels of living induces a low proportion of gains in relation to a high proportion of environmental disamenities and social disbenefits. Moving out along the curve to a position such as I^1 might be taken to represent this condition. Assuming vertical comparability between the p^1-p^2 gap and the new I^1-I^2 gap we can now note that whilst 'goods' still vastly outstrip 'bads' the rate of formation of diseconomies increase, as is shown by the rightward trending of the curve. However, for most medium income countries, the rate of increase in 'goods' so outstrips 'bads' as to make pollution a problem they embrace willingly.

Further along the curve R^1-R^2 represents, for the economically advanced countries, the urbanisation and industrialisation which has led to an excess of pollutants to abate over gains to enjoy. Proponents of growth cite such examples as decentralised electricity generating plants as evidence of a material growth going hand in hand with pollution control (in this case through dilution and dispersal) and to allow for that circumstance, the alternative curve R^1-R^3 has been supplied. The trend to note in both cases is one of markedly less 'goods' in proportion to 'bads' for the economically overdeveloped countries. Thus in the poor country range (p^1-p^2) truly useful articles such as long life cooking pots and cutting tools dominate; in the rich country range ($R^1-R^2R^3$) it is cars and computers. But whereas local technology can be used to fabricate widely used essential consumer products (housing, clothing and food) cars and computers have to be made at specialist plants.

Economic competition and technological facility extends the human depletion of resource endowment far further and with more impact than is biologically acceptable. Pollution characteristics vary as consumer products diversify. The direct consequence of new products are new gases for atmospheric dispersal and new liquids for fluvial discharge, consumer durable products that resist biological degradation, and radioactive and organic toxins which require dense containers and extensive storage space. For the poorer nations the catalogue of material gains appears tantalising, inviting the jibe that for them, if production equals pollution, then it is exactly what they will choose. But there are lessons to be learnt from studying the case history of one country—Japan.

Early in the 1950s, Japan introduced an 'income doubling plan' and by the early 1970s there was 'cornucopia'. Or was there? Heading the list of 'Things you would want the government to do' in a survey was 'Eliminate pollution and public hazards'[2]. Quite clearly, in achieving growth with relatively little regard for their environment, the Japanese induced environmental assaults. It is a feature they would like to reverse; but two factors, one pragmatic the other scientific, are weighed against them. The pragmatic point is that one unit of settled land in Japan already sustains twelve times more economic activity than a comparable unit in the USA, which adds up to spatial and resource constraint.[3] Furthermore, in scientific terms, pollution creates a new ecological order by succession as former high variety ecosystems are replaced by

The 'goods' and 'bads' shown in Diagram 18 showed up the consumption—pollution relationship as less than vital to poor nations and as principally a by-product of consumerism in the economically advanced countries. This new diagram relates to the same subject, 'goods' and 'bads', but the 'bad' is now shown as resource depletion. This shows how the poor, and to a lesser extent the intermediate countries, are exploited through resource depletion.

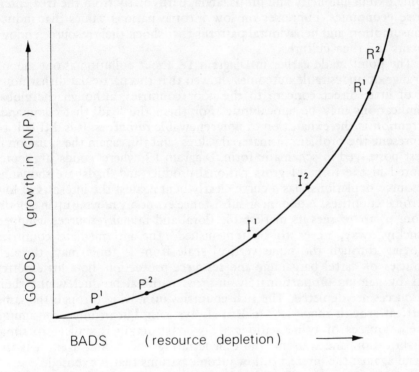

GOODS & BADS Ⅱ

DIAGRAM 19

low variety systems. The Sea of Japan has, for all practical time scales, been altered to its current less lively form and, likewise, the genetic damage to floral and faunal resources through atmospheric pollution is, for practical purposes, new and permanent. Beyond the matter of what might be only a matter of taste or national ambition is the harsher reality that rapid industrialisation induces resource degradation and environmental pollution and contributes to ill health, inadequate housing and the unhappiness of lower paid workers and the unemployed. To some extent publicity and propaganda, particularly from the free enterprise economies, impresses on low income nations values that induce consumption and behavioural patterns that shock their resource endowments and their cultures.

The point made earlier in Diagram 18 about pollution as one among a range of undesirable outcomes showed that this particular disharmony is of little direct concern to the poor countries, although the global implications may be apocalyptic. For them the 'bad' that commands attention is the exhaustion of non-renewable resources. It is difficult to represent the problem in material values, and thus again the situation is best portrayed in schematic form. Diagram 19, where 'goods' are represented in the form of gross national product and 'bads' are shown as resource depletions, has a curve clearly bent against the interests of low income countries. A poor near-subsistence economy moving up in 'goods' from p^1 to p^2 sees its marketable floral and faunal resources whipped quickly away, never to be replenished. The intermediate countries moving through the same vertical scale from I^1 to I^2 may, through policies of cartel bargaining and resource protection, be a little better off by gaining proportionately in gross national product whilst their resources are depleted. The rich countries in moving through the same vertical growth range (R^1 to R^2) always gain, but mainly consuming the resources of other nations. This construction is subject to some qualification and warrants more penetrating review, but again it is the trend against the interest of low income nations that is exposed.

Is there a root to all this? A biologist would wish to affect environmental health and stability by means of biological, ecological and climatic adjustment. Economists proffer classifications such as the World Bank's global, regional and local listing and suggest economic models for growing away from economic and pollution problems.[4] Of course, these are relevant ways to look at the relationship between production and environmental degradation but, as the two previous diagrams show, the poor always come off badly. Resource depletion faces a poor nation if it pursues growth and, if it does attain intermediate status, pollution rates will increase dramatically. But, on balance, resource degradation rather than pollution abatement is the serious issue.

This begs an important question. What is growth and how can its worth be measured? In the case of the USA, nobody would have claimed in 1950 that the average citizen was undernourished, ill housed and inadequately clothed. The same is true today. Americans may eat somewhat different foods, live in different houses and wear rather different clothes but these distinctions are really insignificant, for at both points in time they were well fed, housed and clothed. No-growth here; yet over the same twenty-five years there has been a 130 per cent rise in GNP (against a population increase of 40 per cent) and the average consumption of energy and minerals has climbed astronomically, as this listing of consumer output shows:

> The highest post-war growth rate is the production of non-returnable soda bottles, which has increased about 53,000 per cent in that time. The runners-up are an interesting but seemingly mixed bag. In second place is production of synthetic fibres, up 5,980 per cent; third is mercury used for chlorine production, up 3,120 per cent; air conditioner compressor units, up 2,850 per cent; plastics, up 1,960 per cent; electric housewares (such as can-openers and corn-poppers), up 1,040 per cent; synthetic organic chemicals, up 950 per cent; aluminium, up 680 per cent; chlorine gas, up 600 per cent; pesticides, up 390 per cent . . . . .[5]

The rate of consumption of food, housing, clothing and transportation are much the same now as in 1950, but the methods for fabricating, packaging and transporting these products has greatly altered. Commoner goes on to observe that his average American's

> food is now grown on less land with much more fertiliser and pesticides than before; his clothes are more likely to be made of synthetic fibres than of cotton or wool; he launders with synthetic detergents rather than soap; he lives and works in buildings that depend more heavily on aluminium, concrete, and plastic than on steel and lumber; . . . he drinks beer out of non-returnable bottles or cans rather than out of returnable bottles.[6]

Americans do not all overeat, keep vast wardrobes of clothes or live in palaces, so what is wrong with going about the sustention of life in their way?

We have observed a 40 per cent increase in US population and a 130 per cent increase in GNP, and we know that food, clothing and housing patterns have not changed all that much, but the levels of environmental pollution have risen over the same period at a rate ten times faster than GNP.[7] Furthermore, it is so often the Southern nations which make their resources available for Northern nation consumption. The dizzy heights of American consumerism are well beyond the capacity and ambition of most nations, but were it just possible for some of them to get onto this economic plane the consequences would include global pollution and the ill will created by attempting to command and consume the resources of others. Ward and Dubos claim in *Only One Earth* that Americans now get through the biosphere's supplies at least 500 times faster than people on the Indian sub-continent and in these terms complete global pollution would be the obvious outcome of US levels of consumption for all countries.[8] This point is hypothetical because we know it just cannot happen. Adequate food, clothing and shelter have to be found along a route other than that indicated by Northern models. This route is ecodevelopment, with its emphasis on economic and ecological order whereby resource endowments, climate and population are accepted as the influences which establish, more fundamentally than the latest fashion in economic growth modelling, the course taken to attain an improved present and the best possible future. This may not be economic growth fulfilling but it certainly represents human progress.

Population policy

Is the neo-Malthusian concept of population pollution (i.e. excessive population) emotional or factual? Within human ecosystems disease, natural disaster and human conflict are regulators that have worked effectively to hold human numbers in balance for millennia. In historical terms, many a nation state has followed public health practices, safeguarded its people against invaders and gone out into the world to capture other nations' resources—and been led in the process to form a larger population than their own resource base can support. Decline, sometimes demise, followed. The human disaster is regrettable because of its avoidability.

Consider Diagram 20. Here, excepting this century, it is clearly shown that for most of the previous two thousand years, which one may describe as civilised, the global population pressure on resources has not greatly altered. Bubonic plague, earthquakes, the visitations of Ghengis Khan and the like have, from time to time, worked their awful purpose along with the more commonplace limitations. Yet, surprisingly, they show up as mere blips on the diagram. The perversity is that, now that mankind is able to resist many pathogens and cure most ailments and is doing the same for crops and livestock, the result (as shown in the diagram) is a quadrupling of population from one to four billions in a century. It would be an error to argue that population pollution is not an important issue because it only exists in pockets. The fact is that population and consumption cannot both increase indefinitely from a finite resource base. Thus, even though the human ecosystem is not yet totally overloaded, given the future claims of more poor mouths to feed and more rich consumers to satiate, this condition will surely arise unless corrective measures are taken. If not, the more awful reducing mechanisms such as nuclear war or mono-crop failure will relegate previous influenza epidemics, Sahelian droughts, Bengali floods and world wars to tinkling overtures.

There are three factual measures of overpopulation:

1 When population increase leads to a reduction in the *per capita* availability of basic necessities.

2 When more workers produce less per unit input of labour.

3 When the human environment is persistently impaired.

Thus two material consequences arise from population pollution: namely that the ever increasing number of consumers in low income countries have less to share out, whilst the more static populations of the overdeveloped nations will have to make do with reduced consumption. The concerted global assault that is called for to fight these problems involves population control to replacement (zero population growth) levels in most low income nations and consumer reduction in most materially advanced nations.

Can the already overdeveloped nations lead by example? This is unlikely for they are emasculated by an economic system which clamours for material growth and their failure to regulate population during their own period of industrialisation and colonisation. Control in regard to both consumption and population therefore lies very much with Southern nations. The recent action of raw material producer cartels (OPEC), monopolies (Brazilian coffee) and commodity agreements (tin producers) are examples of consumer limitation.

Population limitation requires that population be 'controlled' to sustain a replacement level which is below the overpopulation threshold. The controls exercised in these instances will be, firstly, a mixture of social sanctions and interventionist contraception in response to economic dictates; and, secondly, abstinence and avoidance in accordance with social pressures. Thus it can be seen that the action taken to limit births occurs at two stages. In the first the influences of religious, cultural and societal institutions are brought to bear. As most religions are dedicated to fostering family life this social benefit approach requires institutional support. Full official support may lag behind, as in South America; or else official policy may run ahead of the financial means to pursue that policy, as in many parts of Asia. This latter problem is often difficult to overcome as funding organisations have been reluctant to give aid (as in India) to birth limitation schemes because of the likely political repercussions.

In the second stage of policy formation all the interruptive methods for controlling the rate of child bearing may be accepted and applied with official sanction. Elements of an initially social, thence progressively

Remorseless extrapolation beyond the present would have the globe a ball of hurtling flesh in a century. One projected absolute limit to human numbers fed, clothed and housed to adequate levels is 16 billions. The 'best fit' recent projection by the World Bank and the United Nations is 7 billions with a levelling off at this figure by the year 2000. This represents an additional 3 billions (mostly in low income areas) over 1980.

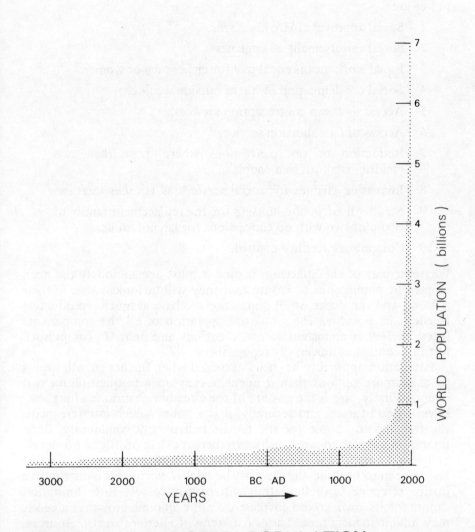

GROWTH IN WORLD POPULATION

DIAGRAM 20

131

socio-economic, contraceptual and finally compulsory birth limitation policy are:

1 Social approval of late marriages.

2 Social endorsement of singleness.

3 Equal work means equal pay for either men or women.

4 Social condemnation of births outside wedlock.

5 Access to cheap contraception services.

6 Access to free abortion services.

7 Reduction of tax concessions where more than two children are born to a couple.

8 Increasing charges for social services as families increase.

9 Standardised public housing for the replacement family of two-plus-two with no concessions for larger families.

10 Compulsory fertility control.

Whatever part of this spectrum is used it must accommodate the need of present populations to ensure that they will be looked after in their old age, and the desire of all populations to have as much reproductive freedom as possible. The wholesale operation of all the components listed as 1—9 is abhorrent in many nations and item 10, compulsory fertility control, is universally repugnant.

Population optimality has been exceeded when further growth begins to close more options than it opens, a view open to question on two counts. Firstly, this is the posture of the already rich ensuring for themselves a good future; and secondly, it is a policy which interferes with the freedom to choose for the female half of any community. Birth limitation appears to work well when there is a clear profile of economic and social benefit for the poor. Distributive justice must be effective and be seen to be done; the corollary being that when there is distributive justice effective birth limitation will readily follow. Birth limitation cannot of its own accord increase overall economic growth; indeed it may inhibit it for a time. The gain in terms of a better share of resources, improved individual health, reduced anxiety and the satisfaction of self-reliance are more important than aggregate scores in the GNP league table.

Consumption limitation brings into effect controls over resource extraction, commodity price agreements, the regulation of patents, the employment of non-nationals and profit taking policies. Poorer countries are understandably eager to take advantage when they have an opportunity to pull these strings for a change. Cartel control is one medium. Non-renewable resources, particularly those in limited supply (such as tin) and those prone to disposal (such as oil) offer more opportunity for cartel fixing than food products such as sugar, coffee, tea and cocoa where consumption has strict limits and for which substitutes or locally grown alternatives can be produced. Other controls involve the pursuit of economic equity through the direct commodity pricing of goods and raw materials which flow from South to North. In a low income context it is important to agree consumer limitation with the rich nations. What this calls for in the Northern nations is an adjustment of prices fair to both exported materials and imported manufactured goods. This will only be achieved when the North directs more of its internal development towards goals of a socially improving rather than a materially aggregating kind.

Employment

The link between employment policy and environment appears tenuous. A review of trends in observable employment brings out the urban and rural, and therefore the environmental dimension to this chronic problem. There is unprecedented growth in the largely urban living labour force arising from the maturity of young people born in the 1960 decade of population explosion. Over the same period there has been a relative reduction of jobs in the modern sector. What is happening is that industrial output is expanding without producing additional jobs.[9] It is generally agreed that the benefits of 'modern', that is manufacturing and public utilities sector expansion (30 per cent in Africa, 34 per cent in Latin America and 44 per cent in Asia)[10] by-pass the rural and traditional employment sectors. This means that the largely urban rich become richer and the rural poor become poorer or stay transfixed. Even in sparsely populated Africa it is the rural sector that harbours this poverty, for some of it to be siphoned off to appear later as urban unemployed.

The humiliation for the unemployed young of having tried, then failed, is bound to whip discontent into political action. Urban accretion in poorer nations is not in balance as was the rural to urban exodus associated with Northern industrialisation; nor, as was the case in those times, can the excess unemployed who wish to work be 'exported' by emigration. All this indicates that sub-national population control must have coherent employment (urban policy) and migration (rural policy) facets.

Urban employment. Basically underemployment, malemployment and unemployment present a problem of finding more worthwhile jobs for an increasing labour force in the face of forms of industrial expansion which demand less labour per unit of production. A common but ineffectual approach to this issue is to increase employment in the tertiary (service) sector by investment in the secondary (manufacturing) sector, and to just accept the 'natural' expansion of automobile minders, bootblackers and lottery ticket vendors.[11] What such lamentably frequent policies induce are accelerating rates of urbanisation during a period of urban expansion that already exceeds all historical precedents.

For a more acceptable solution it is necessary to look at employment as a state reflected in factor endowments. A 'modern sector' injection to the national economy will serve to polarise employment at large urban centres, while a traditional sector redistributive policy will act to decentralise employment opportunities. The main problem in the poorer nations is how to get urban elites to address themselves to the rural factor in primary production; and to accept an accessory role for the urban market economy. If the solution to employment problems is viewed in terms of shifts in economic emphasis then rural and urban equilibrium has to give way to urban convergence. Given low densities of population and a richness of resources, this formula need not be faulted; but high densities of population and a paucity of resources requires that employment policy be related spatially to the national resource endowment.

Education is a key, but it too is urban biased, it being commonplace 'for the population to be growing by 2.5—3.5 per cent per annum, the urban labour force by 6.12 per cent per annum, and the stock of educated persons (with secondary education or above) by 10—15 per cent per annum'.[12] This pattern adds to the urban employment problem in a 'knock on' fashion because modern urban sector production grows faster than the rate at which jobs are created. This results in a growth of educated manpower that cannot find gainful employment. In national terms the urban unemployed represent a problem with no answer, whereas the rural unemployed can, to a greater or lesser extent, be drawn into the productive milieu simply because it is easier to devise labour absorption schemes in rural areas. This point is made in order to stress that primary rural jobs are always usefully productive; conversely, it is the generation of tertiary sector urban jobs that attempt, patronisingly, to make a virtue out of a work, any work, on its own account, yet end up adding disproportionately to overall poverty.

Environmental factors also underscore most of what is registered here against urban proliferation. High natural birth rates, and lack of opportunity in rural areas exacerbate the urban problem, which grows bigger and bigger and just will not go away even if labour reducing technologies and aid monies are hurled into the urban maw. The environmental failings are apparent in the form of consumerism which generates urban misery, pollution and disease. The cause, lack of opportunity in the countryside, must be treated with more vigour than the urban symptoms.

Rural out-migration. Measures of a rural kind to counter rural to urban migratory flows include the family farm (on account of the labour absorption capacities);officially endorsed decentralisation;the equalisation

134

of welfare and educational services between urban and rural localities; the structuring of commodity price equality throughout the spatial framework of a nation, emphasising equality of access to cultural and religious facilities, and the guaranteeing of agricultural prices. These all serve to mollify the 'push' factors in an attempt to align overall policy to a national balance—in particular to stem in-migration to urban areas.

The particular effort made up to 1975 by China to decentralise manufacturing industry is often put forward as an example to heed, although the direct transfer of their concepts is difficult. The decentralisation of health and educational services in China, plus their pursuit of rural self-sufficiency, warrants consideration and some imitation. Rural life is venerated in urban China and the rural population know that they are held in respect by the urban population for their urban sustaining role. It is a position far removed from the elitist urban and industrial emphasis which can be readily identified in centrally directed and market economies alike. What is remarked upon by visitors to rural China is how effectively every person in the community has at least one task to perform that is socially worthwhile and is recognised as such. If the protagonists of growth propulsion measure this as disguised underemployment so be it; but unless they can at the same time show an accretion to human misery or malemployment it matters not a jot. It is precisely when the same measurable condition of underemployment is detected in urban areas in the form of an idle bootblack, the waiting shopkeeper, or the carpenter asleep on his work bench that a more valid cause for concern arises.

A counterpart to the promotion of rural employment involves de-emphasising urban employment as an attractant in its own right. Of course, there are limits because, for example, bicycles cannot be made in cottages. On the other hand, many manufacturing processes aimed at the rural consumer could be decentralised wholly or in part through official policies and controls. If the aim is to take manufacturing to the people, then governments may choose to tax large scale manufacturing processes whether it be to fabricate soap or sewing machines; and to sustain this policy in order to attain an employment balance in the face of claims for economies of scale, price reductions and better quality control. Taxing scale has been mentioned as one decentralising ploy; tax concessions as an incentive to decentralise is another; free site incentives are another; and rent subsidies and tax holidays are others. All this can be done to reduce the urban dole queue, thereby inducing people, without coercion of a feudal kind, to stay close to the soil. These are the carrots and sticks of regional policy. More specifically rural policies further demand the creation of equal opportunity of access to public services, schools, hospitals and communication facilities. The urban corollary to rural advocacy involves downgrading the emphasis upon a centralised transfer of resources whereby urban services and benefits are funded from the rural tax base, coupled to an insistence that equality of access rather than urban centrality determine the provision of social, medical and educational services.

Concluding comment

The impact of resource consumption and population growth is measured by detecting whether the depletion of resources and accretions of population results in material and social benefit or disadvantage. In a few rare examples (Brazil being one) more people can mean an increase in material living standards for a time; but for most low income nations resource scarcity will usually result in the same or a reducing quantity of resources being shared by a greater number of people. Population limitation policy has an interface with resource utilisation policy which may be gauged materially in terms of human consumption and expressed socially in terms of human satisfaction. It is in this way that population and resource consumption policies are as closely bound to material and social progress as is economic planning. A burgeoning population can simply render impressive economic growth rate meaningless.

Notes

1   Frederick Stoddy, *Matter and Energy*, Williams and Norgate, London, 1912.

2   J.W. Bennett, Sukehiro Hesegawa and S.E. Levine, 'Japan', *Environment*, vol.15, no.10, December 1973, Table 3 — 61% support.

3   Bennett et al., loc.cit., p.7.

4   World Bank Group, *Environment and Development*, World Bank, Washington, 1975.

5   Barry Commoner, *The Closing Circle*, Jonathan Cape, London, 1972, p.143.

6   Commoner, loc.cit., p.145.

7   Commoner, loc.cit., p.146.

8   Barbara Ward and Rene Dubos, *Only One Earth*, Penguin Books, London, 1972, p.176.

9   Reported from a United Nations source, 'The Growth of World Industry' by K. Geoffrey in *Development and Underdevelopment*, MacMillan, London, 1975, p.127.

10 David Turnham and Ingelies Jaeger, *The Employment Problems in Less Developed Countries*, OECD, Paris, 1971, p.10.

11 An explanation can be modelled in accordance with queuing theory applied in relation to job prospects which works in a way comparable to the decision an individual might take to join or not to join a queue for a popular movie knowing that by the time he or she gets near the head of the queue it may be too late. As an explanation this model is neat, but it fails to indicate any solution to the urban employment problem.

12 Richard Jolly, Emanuel de Kald, Hans Singer and Fiona Wilson, *Third World Employment*, Penguin Education, London, 1973, p.17.

7 The economics of ecodevelopment

> The efficiency of an economic system is not a
> quantity but a ratio.
>
> *Lewis Mumford, 1933*[1]

Nations cannot wipe out unemployment simply by switching on neo-classical, moneterist or centrally directed development models because, for the desired effect to be achieved, these all call for something like a 20 per cent compounding increase in energy consumption to sustain a 5 per cent compounding increase in economic growth.[2] The critical minimum effort required to produce so much planned social surplus is beyond capacity. This is fact. Almost as certain, and definitely more significant from an environmental viewpoint, political and administrative systems (the broad expression of economic systems) are not easily able to turn away from policies which stress monetary growth toward that alternative which aims for progress and improvement through eco-development.

The economics of development

Despite problems of comparability, the notion of a monetary measure-ment of poverty in terms of income *per capita* (usually gross national product or gross national expenditure) is the one still most frequently used. Diagram 21 is a depiction along these lines. A common line used to divide the already developed and low income nations is US$200 *per capita* in each year—but for the poorer countries purchasing power

At the outset (Chapter 1 and Diagram 1) an effort was made to express the North–South distinction in non-monetary terms. Now, in this chapter, the subject is the economies of ecodevelopment, and an economic classification of the 100 countries with more than 2.5 million population is made. However, aggregates of this kind can be very mischievous; Nepal and Chad equate numerically, as do China and Kenya, but the distribution of misery and wellbeing differ greatly in each set. Nevertheless, there is a correlation between this diagram and Diagram 1.

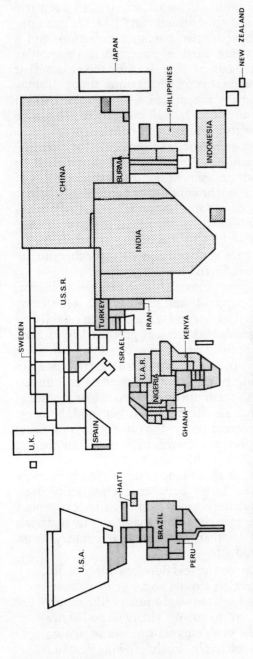

CLASSIFICATION OF 100 COUNTRIES

ADVANCED   30% **of World Population**
[More than $1000 per capita income per annum]

INTERMEDIATE   15% **of World Population**
[$200 - $1000 per capita income per annum]

POOR   55% **of World Population**
[Less than $200 per capita income per annum]

NORTH

SOUTH

Choroplethic Presentation – displayed map area of each country is in proportion to the number of inhabitants.

DIAGRAM 21

141

elasticities coupled to the varying extent of trade in kind ensures that a spending power of say $150 per annum in Nepal, will lead to a remarkably more satisfactory life than the same amount in Chad, for example. This is understood. The real point is that human satisfaction, and a balanced utilisation of resources, are parts of an ecological reckoning which has, so far, defied monetary comparison. It is for this reason that the zero growth concept is not attractive, well meaning though it may be. Numerical or monetary growth is acceptable when a nation can get it. More important is the identification of overall progress which can be expressed in terms of health, security, comfort and convenience.

Money, of its own accord, is best regarded as a surrogate for quantitative material value. It is one manifestation of an institution used to facilitate exchange between goods and services and to express stores of value. It has these powers by virtue of the confidence peoples and nations place in it. This understanding of money, more as a shadow than a substance, is keenly perceived by 'Fourth World' resource rich countries. Here money supply induces a mischief by becoming an artefact of a price system in which the confidence is placed above those other institutions and values which previously reflected human prosperity.

The recipients of 'new' money, and money which is being recirculated, go to the market place to purchase goods and services with a faith that the cash paid for their own personal labour and services has an established exchange value relative to the goods and services produced by others. Provided this confidence is maintained and resources do not become scarce, all will be well. What we now know is that the extra money in circulation undermines purchasing power confidence. And this undermining puts an ever increasing cash premium on non-renewable resources (particularly fossil fuels) which has an effect on all other food, housing, clothing, transportation and construction costs. Taking aid and giving credit do little to adjust the proportional distribution of the purchasing power; certainly, never from the rich to the poor.

This monetary connotation is worth looking at more closely in a low income context. In the act of exchange between economically overdeveloped and economically underdeveloped countries an exogenous merchant takes a profit at home as a cheap purchaser of raw materials from a poor nation, then takes another profit in that country as an expensive vendor of furnished products.

> What developed countries say to the less developed is broadly along these lines: 'If you care to export to us primary commodities which we need and which we do not produce ourselves—then please feel free to do so. We shall put no barrier in your way and your only problems will be those arising from price instability and a relatively slowly growing demand (partly caused by our capability and interest in producing synthetic substitutes)—which means that you will probably

have to export larger and larger quantities to pay for any given volume of imports of our manufactures. You can't, of course, expect us to be quite so liberal with regard to those primary products which we can, if only by offering subsidies, sometimes produce ourselves. If, however, you decide to hedge against these difficulties by processing yourselves some of the raw materials which would otherwise have been sent to us, then we're afraid that some disincentive is called for. Duty will be payable on such imports.'[3]

A dramatic example was tea production in pre-independence Ceylon, where the plantations were foreign owned and whose production was sold to foreign tea traders. The traders shipped the tea in foreign owned craft to London where the purchasers bought, blended and sold to dealers who took some of the same tea back to Ceylon for sale to foreign owned storekeepers, who closed the circle by taking a final profit from the producing labourer! Each step of the exchange had a profit element which fell to the external agent. Market forces, left alone, ensure that low income areas retain low monetary status as a basic resource supplier whilst the Northern nations control capital, technology and marketing.[4]

It can be argued that the global rate of development has been relatively constant since the Second World War, but a poor country growing at the same rate as a rich country derives much lower *per capita* increments because of the lower base from which growth started. Hopes for economic comparability are thus misfounded because of the widening gap between rich and poor regions. Add to this dismal scene increases in population, and it can be clearly shown that economic growth as a development ideal has given no relative advantage or improvement to low income countries in the North—South exchange, whereas the scope for progress, partly measured in resource distribution and environmental conservation, is enormous.

Distribution from growth

A case can be made for attaining a general policy for equity through a related policy of redistribution, preferably from growth. The presumption is that the overdeveloped agree to distribute goods to the underdeveloped: but when aid targets to distribute as little as 2 per cent of GNP are not being met by the overdeveloped countries, it is clear that the actual amount redistributed is not significant. Distribution from growth is impaled partly because of neglect by overdeveloped nations, and also because of the gross disparity between the rich and poor within low income countries themselves. An attempt to express this condition is given in Diagram 22.

For the majority of people in low income areas, the basis of liveli-

Diagram 2 in the Introduction showed up the unacceptable imbalance between Northern and Southern nations trading on a global scale. The Lorenz curve given here   for the low income countries is conjectural. It shows the unacceptable imbalance of income distribution within low income nations. The global imbalances can only partly be held to mutually assimilate national imbalances—in other words, within country adjustments are just as much a part of progressive development proposals as are the adjustment of commodity transfer trade offs.

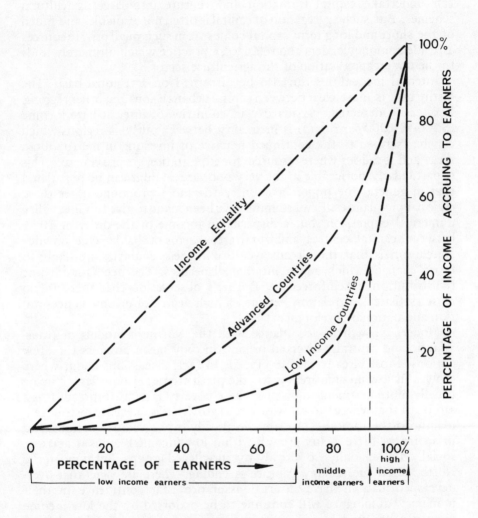

MODEL FOR INCOME DISTRIBUTION

DIAGRAM 22

145

hood is agriculture, and here it can be noted that tropical produce is relatively inelastic as to price, and the margin of excess that can be aggregated in the form of personal savings from agricultural incomes is always small. Therefore, in these countries, it is only government that can undertake capital formation and venture into large agricultural schemes. But such aggregation of capital is often not available, and much of the short and long term capital comes from such small private sources as traders, moneylenders and relatives; a practice which ultimately leads to the undercapitalisation of the agriculture sector.

Internal inequalities can also be discerned on a regional basis. The distinction is most clear between capital urban regions and other regions. Less easily detected, particularly in countries of intermediate income ($200–$1,000 *per capita*) is inequality between outlying regions which can be ascribed to the continued practice of investing in metropolitan areas and localities where resources for exploitation are proximate.[5] This is particularly noticeable in the very poor areas and it can be postulated that in general the poorer a country the more pronounced are these regional inequalities. Few attempts have been made to give this inequality numerical expression, but a disparity in income of the order of 10–1 between capital centres and rural areas seems probable. One obvious conclusion is that the already wealthy in these countries are likely to resist changes which adjust internal disparities. The need for income redistribution is reinforced by Dorner's observation that there is 'no close statistical correlation between a high degree of income concentration and national development'.[6]

Modern growth in accordance with the Northern models of trans-atlantic and centrally directed origin can only mean progress for a few nations—those already overdeveloped. In fact, discussions about where growth in low income areas is to take place are rather pointless, it being usually more pertinent to discuss where poverty is next to spread. It is a sad truth that where there is widespread growth it is unevenly distributed, mainly to the capital centres in the already overdeveloped nations, and in so far as there is any growth within low income regions it accrues, socially and spatially, to already overprivileged groups. But now, in the North, fossil fuel energy capture is ending. There are signs that over-developed nations have no real assurance that confidence in their monetary dominance will continue to be endorsed by the low income countries. In fundamental terms, growth can only be produced from natural resources and here the economically underdeveloped countries have some fortune, for today they are the resource endowed, especially with regard to climate, and so often they harbour impressive stocks of renewable and non-renewable resources.

Attempts to institute perpetual economic motion in the form of money based incentive systems are written indelibly on the now arid landscapes of several fallen civilisations in temperate and tropical regions.

146

Historians more frequently belabour moral and institutional decay than the lessening of economic returns squeezed from deteriorating endowments, but the ruined landscapes of Mesopotamia in the distant past and of the Dust Bowl yesteryear are abundantly clear.[7] These lessons from experience have not been greatly heeded, partly because of the lack of communication across the oceans separating the low income tricontinent and partly because these disasters largely missed the temperate zones in their separate progress via the colonisation of other peoples' labour and resources. But now population numbers, global resource demand and what can be described as interdependence is more advanced and more delicately balanced; and it can be observed that the scale of disaster arising from threshold strain of an ecological kind has increased in geographical extent and affects more people. The fundamental relationship can still be identified as that between man and land; but the key, as it were, is largely held by the incorporeal money incentive system which has previously served to advance consumption and urbanise people away from the land. When a money system fails to support continuous growth, profits are replaced by losses, insufficiency replaces consumerism and austerity arises to replace prosperity.

What has been established is that, in terms of average income per head, the prospects in most low income countries would not be hopeful even if relatively high rates of economic growth were sustained because appreciable numbers cannot benefit from this form of growth. The principle of pareto approved utility should be used to ensure that any development carried out increases individual or group wellbeing without making some other person or group worse off. More simply expressed, a pareto approved utility would be represented by a flattening of the income distribution curve given in the previous diagram.

In seeking an explanation for the depressed economic base in low income countries, it is necessary to look to the trade policies of the transatlantic and centrally directed Northern nations, their promotion of dependency, demographic upsurges in the disease ridden tropics, social hindrances and distributional imbalances. It is a matter of inextricable complexity to explain differential rates of development measured by monetary criteria for different people living in somewhat varied environments. Furthermore, what signifies development? Is Peru at about $800 GNP *per capita* annum more 'developed' than Northern China at about $400? This is, in part, a problem arising from a growth fixation upon gross national product. In fact, up to 1972, the GNP growth rate for most of the medium income countries was about the same as for the economically more advanced; but during that same period the rate of population growth in the wealthy nations was very low (at around 0.2 to 1.5 per cent) whilst it was usually over 2 per cent in the poorer countries (see Table 3).

Another factor to consider is that of outflow of profits from external investment in low income countries. Thus it is in the poorer nations that the effects of free play market forces and population controls, both tenets beloved by believers of incentive systems, can be observed first-hand. It is apparent that the capitalist ideal of each to his worth drives, in the market place of these countries, a cruel, constantly reinforced wedge between profiteers and social outcasts.[8]

Progress in lieu of growth

Progress is sanctioned by the pareto principle in that there are no losers and there are always some who gain welfare utility; in this case, a utility not necessarily synonymous with economic growth. Likewise, the economic poverty of people with few possessions does not mean that they are materially poor for their environment may be kindly and healthy, their shelter and clothing needs well met and they may feel socially secure. This cannot be described as 'poverty'. The use of the term as an indicator of social deprivation can be held to be a material concept arising from socialist and capitalist schools of thought. Both accede to the belief that social standing is a function of economic determinism and both are equally doctrinaire about the labour theory of value, whereas ecodevelopment would set about price controlling all natural and human resources. Growth in wealth is seen by the socialist and capitalist schools to be the only way by which poverty can be 'bought' out—indeed socialist planners often claim faster than capitalist rates of growth for their models. Poor countries should be cautious about heeding the opinions of the already overdeveloped regarding their 'poverty' and be particularly wary of mischievous and largely discredited growth perspectives such as that given in Table 6 which is derived in part from Rostow, but is also reflected in the earlier work on regional and urban planning by John Friedman.[9]

The last component in this model, the drive to maturity, is historic-ally identifiable within the now overdeveloped economies. The compli-cation for contemporary low income nations seeking this kind of purely economic advance today is that they fail to consolidate stage three, the stage of economic take off. This suggests that, given contemporary North —South competitiveness, stage three is (excepting resource endowed countries) unobtainable. At this stage, according to the standard explanation of the failure of these countries to take off, difficulties over balance of payments and inflation arise, stemming from the need to pay for their overcapitalisation from the humble service tax base, resulting in a downward spiral effect which is further reflected in a proportional increase in unemployment. All these factors, naturally, are compounded as population increases. This is in many ways an oversimplification, but it serves to highlight just where poverty might be overcome, by both

148

improving the nutritional quality of food intake and limiting the rate of population growth within an ecodevelopment framework. The most beneficial approach to both policies is to work toward a unified commitment to resource and population planning at the optimum pace of social and administrative transition. However, the more usual practice is to seek ostentatious growth through big projects as the central and often the sole policy.

A study from the Organisation for Economic Co-operation and Development shows that to reduce unemployment to 5 per cent, low income countries would need an hypothetical (that is, population unconstrained) 7 per cent minimum increment in growth rates.[10] This is clearly difficult. Arthur Lewis expressed the same objective in the first development decade when he called for the reinvestments of 12–15 per cent of income to overcome poverty.[11] Such increases in output and ploughback cannot be sustained from any resource base and thus, in terms of this constraint, Lewis' policy constituted a flight of economic fancy. What is questionable is whether the extant living conditions observed in these studies really constituted material poverty. If poverty is perceived in any particular country then the solution should not be seen to lie in economic growth *per se* but in the increase of nutritional uptake, in improvements to the habitat, and in the equitable distribution of the goods of production. These criteria vary greatly between different habitats. Equity in the distribution of the goods of production means fundamentally and first, a more fair distribution of current production; and if there is overall growth (say, by introducing higher yielding varieties into agriculture) then this too must be fairly distributed. It has other ramifications. For example, more efficient production in technical or monetary terms may have to be eschewed because widespread unemployment, underemployment and malemployment are criteria as valid in measuring perceived poverty as scarcity of cash.

Modernisation, in the sense of begetting industry, only generates employment at a rate about equal to a third of the rate of increase in economic growth, which makes it the kind of progress most of the poorer nations could do without.[12] This predicates a modest rate of capitalisation per workplace: in the case of agriculture something roughly equal to prevailing *per capita* GNP, and for industrial capitalisation, maybe twice that. This further suggests that greater emphasis should be laid on agriculture rather than industry simply because more workplaces are 'earned' from investment in agriculture than industry. This approach characterises poverty alleviation policies which emphasise progress more than growth.

Table 6

Monetary growth delusion: Rostow's model for low income countries

Leading economic activity	Rowstow stage	Era	% of population	
			Rural	Urban
Subsistence farming coupled to hunting and fishing		Pre-colonial	100	–
Exploitation of valuable accessible minerals	Traditional society —the colonial era	1700—1900	98	2
Colonial plantation agriculture		1800—1940	85	15
Exploitation of a massive mineral deposit (oil, gold, copper, etc.) *or* large scale development of a plantation crop (cocoa, coffee, sugar, rubber, etc.)	Precondition for take off	1930—1950	70	3
Import substitution and the development of an industrial base	Take off	1950—1980	60	40
Export drive from an industrial base	Maturity	1980+	50	50

External diseconomies

It is now received wisdom that the use of capital as the seed of growth leads to a rapid exploitation of renewable resources, the near depletion of some non-renewable resources, and the dispersal of residual pollutants beyond tolerable limits. Thus the relationship between poverty, resource utilisation and pollution becomes clear. Three important interconnected elements can be identified:

1 The economic cost of recycling or disposing of residuals in accordance with controls or taxes is seen by primary and secondary producers as an externality of production to be avoided whenever possible. This is clear by the curve shown as the 'cost of pollution control to industry' in Diagram 23. The other curve establishes pollution, during the manufacturing stage, as a negative, exponentially increasing (absorptive) input to an economy.

2 Whether the cost of recycling or disposing residuals is met by the manufacturer, the consumer or society at large, there arises a monetary diseconomy (the abatement cost) which has to be met and which appears in the gross national expenditure ledger, erroneously, as adding to wealth and growth.

3 Arithmetic increases in resource utilisation result in something like a geometrical increase in residuals generation as a community cost for absorption. In other words, as growth in resource utilisation increases 1, 2, 3, 4, 5, the rate of residuals disposal increases, possibly as 1, 2, 4, 8, 16. Diagram 24 shows this latter relationship.

The diseconomies of residuals absorption are relatively minor in poor countries and in most of the intermediate income countries. As secondary production goes up, the community price that has to be paid for these consumer benefits also increases, but exponentially. Not only has the price of pollution inexorably to be paid but, in the absence of safeguards, it will be paid largely by those very underprivileged whom all honest governments would want to assist. This indicates that intermediate countries, in particular, should undergo a fundamental rethink before they adopt the industrial development model. The evils of low cost labour extortion and resource exploitation may be foreseen and avoided by uncorrupted politicians; but what their modern economic advisors fail to stress is that, in the terms just argued, the consumer benefits of growth are not justified when they fall to an already privileged minority (such as themselves) leaving abatement costs as a burden upon the whole community.

Money values have dominated the examination so far. This system of

Pollution abatement costs have to be met either by the producers or the community (including all consumers) at large—and generally by a combination of both. Before exhorting the productive benefits of industrial growth, it is as well to realise that these two costs must be discounted from profits in order to arrive at a true image of the worth of an industrial enterprise.

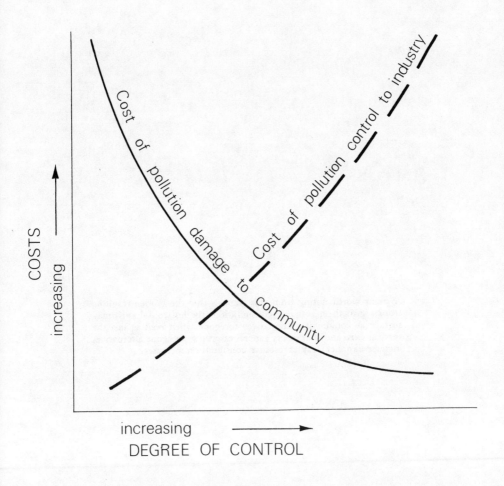

THE DISTRIBUTION OF POLLUTION
COST - BURDENS

DIAGRAM 23

A point worth noting from this graph is that the burden resulting from a growth in resource consumption (the horizontal axis) may surface as community alternatives foregone when read against the vertical axis; and that in any general case these foregone alternatives increase exponentially as resource consumption increases.

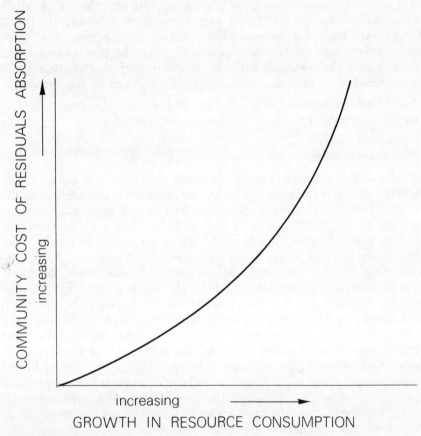

COMMUNITY COST OF RESIDUALS ABSORPTION

increasing

increasing

GROWTH IN RESOURCE CONSUMPTION

BURDEN SHARING OF RESIDUALS ABSORPTION

DIAGRAM 24

155

value measurement has some validity, but damage to the environment dramatically illustrates external diseconomies to the community. Business enterprises brought into being to produce monetary profits are not bound to depart from policies which demand, as a working principle, the discard of residuals with minimum effect upon profit margins. Material damage will result simply because manufacturing processes of all resource consuming kinds involves the conversion of matter to goods and residuals. The new forms these converted resources will take vary from some high utility consumer goods to toxic wastes. These arise as a consequence of processing and manufacturing which involve the conversion of matter into consumption 'goods' for profit plus residual 'bads' for disposal. The point to stress again is that commercial enterprises operate in accordance with the profit motive and are concerned almost solely with the production of consumption goods and services for profit. Two contrasting equations can be generated:

$$\text{Gross national product (high money value)} = \text{Goods and services } plus \text{ costs of residuals absorption}$$

$$\text{Consumer goods (low mass volume)} = \text{Resource mass } less \text{ residuals mass}$$

With the latter, environmentally focussed equation, the mass of consumption goods is far outweighed by the residuals mass; whereas in the first equation the monetary value that can be put upon consumption goods far outweighs the value of the residuals. This is the development paradox: more consumption in monetary terms results in a more than proportional increase in negative value wastes for disposal.

There are some further implications. A first is that industrial manufacturing and exploitative mining have the highest ratio, by mass, of 'bads' to 'goods', and few low income countries avoid the attendant earth moving ravages and ore refining waste disposal problems. A second implication is that discharges of unprofitable heat, liquid toxins and harmful gases lead to other forms of social disbenefits such as work injuries and occupational diseases. A third is that agriculturally biased economies can avoid these negative social effects more effectively than industrial nations and, although this is a considerable environmental benefit for them, their feelings about missing out on the 'benefits' of industrialisation also need to be understood.

Resource conversion leads to the manufacture of some useful goods of limited mass (and high value) together with a high mass of relatively useless residuals. This raises a consideration of where these useless residuals are to be dumped, the crux here being the matter of private and common property rights. A strip mining enterprise may heft the overburden about on its own estate leaving behind a moonscape when mineral exploitation is finished, and provided this disposal takes place on private property it may be tolerated by society; but it would not be

156

expected that mineral acid discharged into common property, such as a river flowing out of the estate, could be accepted as the exercise of an untramelled right. Residuals do not disappear when desirable goods have been derived, they are dispersed as solids on the landscape; as liquids and solids into the river and marine systems; and as gases into the atmosphere.

Sometimes such assimilation raises little concern; but modern manu-facturing processes create bulk residuals, and some lesser discharges that are very harmful indeed. Furthermore, the rate of increase in the discharge of the less easily assimilated residuals increases at a faster rate than the rate of increase in *per capita* income, thereby inducing a more pronounced backward loop in the previous diagram. There is an unseen hand waiting to tax the abatement due for every material gain, and poorer countries should consider this 'cost' before seeking industrial growth for its own sake. These benefits and disbenefits must be weighed up in deciding on the balance to be struck between agriculture, mineral exploitation and industrialisation.

Increases in profit can be outstripped by increases in the costs of abatement and clean-up. Thus if the capital enterprise instrument of monetary gain is harnessed to resources, proportional increases in profits will be matched by a compounding increase in the costs of residuals absorption. The profit motive is deeply entrenched. It is only when it is put into review against development ambitions (whether free enterprise or socialist) that seek to establish progress in material terms, that waste looms to defeat the benefits of profit, even if some few individuals benefit. The course open to governments is to provide a means whereby the owners of enterprises producing waste heat, liquids, gases and solids can be persuaded, coerced or forced (if necessary) to avoid official ridicule in the pursuit of monetary gains which impose external dis-economies upon society. They can achieve this by paying compensatory taxes, or simply by intervening in the residuals producing processes. In doing so, the initial 50 per cent of abatement can usually be achieved at low cost (often about 3 per cent of production cost) whereas 70 per cent clean-up may cost twice as much and 80 per cent four times as much. From an official point of view, the main problem is which system of enforcement, taxes or regulations, should be used. Consumer emitted pollution such as fumes from a motor vehicle are generally best kept in check by means of regulative devices backed up by powers to prosecute and fine offenders, with an increase in penalty for persistent or serious contravention. With producer emitted pollution such as the discharge of liquid factory wastes into a marine system, the better approach is to tax the discharge, with an inversely reducing rebate for producers who take the initiative to organise abatement and clean-up.

Only recently have the private gains self-evidently prescribed in the economic policies of those who believe nations can grow out of their material poorness (Friedman, Johnson)[13] been balanced against the social losses outlined by the 'progress' school (Galbraith and Mischan).[14] What is now clear in the already overdeveloped nations is that the individual monetary gains of economic growth may be outweighed by the price communities have to pay for damage to the common property resources into which producers, and individuals as consumers, discharge wastes. This springs from the premise that, in terms of any individual's notion of efficiency, common property resources will be exploited whilst there is some margin of gain to be extracted from so doing, even when the accumulated community price that has to be paid is higher than the individual's benefit. For poorer countries this holds equally true: the rich consume more and seek to consume yet more again while the poor subsist, become environmentally polluted, and in the normal case do not stand to gain proportionally from the expansion of production. Yet a cautionary perspective should be held, for whatever social inequities can be detected in the low income nations the problem of common property resource pollution is, in aggregate, nowhere near as serious there as it is in the materially advanced countries. In low income areas the trend to be curbed is the exploitation of renewable resources such as soils, flora and fauna which heap more riches on those few who are already well off rather than the population at large.

Property rights in relation to all resources, including those in private ownership, plus definitions of the right to use resources and to discharge residuals into common property and upon private land: this is the important policy lynchpin to the resolution of the conflict between ecological virtues and economic values. Another is that growth policies inevitably result in the inequitable distribution of gains. To go into a future where more growth is intended for more people as the professed objective is theoretically laudable; but for the rural poor in low income countries the actual outcome of such a policy is far less optimistic. Clearly a new order derived in part from environmental concern is called for to ensure that progress through ecodevelopment rather than monetary growth policies prevail.

Concluding comment

This chapter advanced the thesis that it is better for the governments of low income nations to contemplate the realities of human progress in preference to the illusion of economic growth. Whereas economic growth for Southern nations is desirable but illusive, social improvement is very possible. Human progress of this kind has minimum criteria; namely for all individuals to be adequately fed, appropriately sheltered and comfortably clothed; for non-renewable resources to be fully and fairly won and for renewable resources to be carefully husbanded; and in general that human dignities and rights be observed. The attainment of objectives of this kind really is gainful. Views along these lines are at odds with the opinions of those who campaign for growth through economic expansion. But what they fail to realise is that, from the level of the poor populace, private capital is seen to chase paper money profits. Of itself this may not be intrinsically bad, and anyway it is the prerogative of any government to inhibit or encourage the profit motive as it sees fit; but external investment equates with exported profits and this is a detraction from the notion of human progress. Capitalisation and aid can do very little to promote progress--indeed they demonstrably support urban and industrial bias, whet the consumer appetite beyond its resource support capacity and generate economic and political enclaves of privilege. Internal capitalisation coupled to a sensitive regulation of money supply is more desirable in that it creates low cost workplaces and the taking of profits at home.

What I have set down is inhibitive where it refers to taxes and restrictive when it refers to regulations. I am, however, not so much against economic growth as for emphasising and upgrading ecodevelopment as a broadly based form of overall social progress; and I advocate achieving this more through the use of political and institutional power than through the manipulation of economic factors. I am, therefore, optimistic about human progress in low income areas; although I am somewhat pessimistic about the future for Northern nations.

In bypassing economic growth and the industrialisation model, the poor regions will not miss the illusory benefits of monetary expansion as they move toward widespread improvement through ecodevelopment. Indeed, I believe that Northern nations will eventually be obliged to take a cue from the South, thereby setting more conventional development assumptions on their head.

Notes

1   Lewis Mumford, from *Findings and Keepings,* Secker and Warburg, New York, 1975, p.27.

2   Gerald Foley, *The Energy Question,* Penguin Books, London, 1976, p.265.

3   Peter Donaldson, *Worlds Apart: the Economic Gulf Between Nations,* Penguin Books, London, 1973, p.141.

4   The role of merchant capital in development is systematically analysed by K. Geoffrey in *Development and Underdevelopment,* (chapter on merchant capital and underdevelopment), Macmillan Press, London, 1975.

5   In Ghana, for example, I found (1973) that the five peripheral regions with 68 per cent of the land and 50 per cent of the population commanded 12 per cent of the budgeted funds, whilst Accra capital district, with 1 per cent of the land coverage and 7 per cent of the population commanded the other half.

6   Peter Dorner, *Land Reform and Economic Development*, Penguin Books, London, 1972, p.83.

7   These and many other examples are presented from a US establishment point of view by V.G. Carter and T. Dale in *Topsoil and Civilisation*, Oklahoma Press, (revised edition), 1976.

8   Amin gives some figures 'which are rarely quoted'; thus in West Africa 'the rate of growth in this outflow of profits (3.8 per cent a year) has been higher than the growth in the gross contribution of private foreign capital (3.2 per cent a year)'. Samir Amin, *Neo Colonialism in West Africa*, Penguin African Library, London, 1973, p.271.

9   W.W. Rostow, *The Stages of Economic Growth*, Cambridge University Press, Cambridge, 1961; John Friedman, *Regional Development Policy*, MIT Press, Cambridge, Mass., 1966, Table 6.1. Further to this, in 1973, by which time the 'Stages of Growth' notion was being regarded rather suspiciously, Friedman set down the hopeful view that, 'Countries in the early phases of industrialisation must make spatial integration the overriding policy objective; they are still striving to achieve a minimum measure of national unity. At a later stage regional inequities become predominant and will have to be balanced against the requirement of efficiency in location. Still later, well into the post-industrial period of development, policy objectives for urbanization will be primarily concerned with questions of environmental quality and the structure and organization of major metropolitan regions.' John Friedman, *Urbanization Planning and National Development*, Sage Publications, Beverley Hills, 1973, p.137.

10   David Turnham (assisted by Ingelies Jaeger), *The Employment Problem in Less Developed Countries*, OECD, Paris, 1971, p.116.

11   W. Arthur Lewis, *Development Planning*, Allen and Unwin, London, 1968.

12   Secondary source, from Harbison, *The Generation of Employment*, Kericho Conference, University of Nairobi, 1966.

13   Milton Friedman, *Capitalism and Freedom*, 1962; Harry G. Johnson (died 1977), *Man and His Environment*, 1973.

14   J. Kenneth Galbraith, *A Contemporary Guide to Economics Peace and Laughter*, 1971; and E. Mishan, *Economic Growth Debate*, 1977.

8 Technological reform

> What an irony it would be if this most enlightened, civilized and powerful generation of human beings should through their own greed, blindness and neglect, bring about the end of the human experiment.
>
> *Maurice Strong, 1975*[1]

> Tenderly now, lethal man, turn to the earth.
>
> *Ansel Adams, 1964*[2]

The technological reforms which ecodevelopment presages also bring us to a trilogy of apparently mutually excluding ideals—modernity, self-sufficiency and appropriateness. With the exception of some localities where feudal overlordship and religious bigotry still hold, most low income nations aspire to be more modern and as self-sufficient as possible. Most nations also see an appeal in their 'appropriate' use of local knowledge and resources. Thus the trilogy is not really mutually excluding, and technological reforms can embrace modernity, self-sufficiency and appropriateness. Modernisation and self-sufficiency are clear. It is the concept of appropriateness that has to be explored more fully.

What is economically and environmentally appropriate to Northern nations is not necessarily mirrored in the Southern world. Indeed, the most massive impediment to technological appropriateness is the Northern nation industrial model. Thus technological appropriateness

161

in low income countries is determined by establishing the economic and environmental principles that fit societal concerns to be modern and self-sufficient. Economic and environmental appropriateness is, therefore, bound together with national ambitions to be progressively modern and to acquire independent capabilities.

A conceptual framework to which technological appropriateness can be attached has already been set down as 'policy guidelines' in Chapter 5. This constitutes a rejection of the view that the poorer nations have no alternative development model, and from it can be deduced the two main reasons which establish the case for socially, economically and environmentally appropriate technology. The first is that such an approach conserves the regenerative capacity of renewable resources and utilises non-renewable resources to benefit all society; and the second is that it more fully employs local skills and local capital thereby reducing external dependence. Just how appropriately technology is applied is very largely a consequence of the strength of political conviction and commitment, but structurally it is of two orders. This has been expressed by Qurashi as embodied and unembodied technology.[3]

Embodied technology radiates out 'horizontally' from a local technological base (for example the elaboration of tube-well technology in Pakistan) whereas unembodied technology is imposed 'vertically' from external technological sources (as is usual with communications technology). The distinction facilitates understanding yet it is not particularly helpful for, whilst unembodied technology may be intended to emancipate, it often only rewards the already privileged and reinforces the hardship of the already underprivileged. The same argument can hold against the so-called enlightened use of local technologies. Nevertheless, the embodied or unembodied distinction is structurally useful. From it we can pursue the principle of appropriateness in the social, economic and environmental guises of ecodevelopment. This calls for the identification of technologies that are adaptive and good, plus recognition of technologies that are environmentally non-adaptive, economically unsound and socially questionable.

Politics and technological choice

A technological fix for material comfort is as remote from reality as increased GNP is from social progress. But, unlike profit, the choice of technology can very largely be decided internally within an economy. Technology is, thereby, a major political factor in any nation's development policy. It is a part of political ecology which will cause decision makers to decide what products and what manufacturing processes should be encouraged and to what locally acceptable standards. Such decisions may fly in the face of established external trade patterns and decision taking procedures; they are, therefore, very political indeed.

Historical evidence teaches that technology can be environmentally adaptive. After all, it served to put off the Malthusian doomsday for many by increasing the production rate of agriculture as well as improving the processing, storage and, distribution of foodstuffs. This was certainly the case of the now economically advanced countries in temperate zones. But in the tropics large scale technological innovation is often non-adaptive. It is for this reason that we find that smaller powered machinery such as the paddy tillers in use throughout South East Asia are well suited, environmentally, to rice culture in that their use shows no serious sign of hastening soil erosion or exhaustion in circumstances where large scaled agricultural machinery would be impractical and environmentally damaging. Hydrological technology has also served the temperate zones rather better than the tropical arid lands, where there are unexpected environmental changes, soil salination, waterborne disease distribution and silting problems.

Claims that technology is politically neutral must be rejected. New or altered technologies always change the ecosystem, the social system and the economic system; and it is only with a knowledge of this certainty that technological reform can be considered. There is no technological fix to adopt, but there are some technological myths to allay.

The improving notion

Technological reform is not a matter of high thinking resulting in improved living. One view of appropriate technology is that it is deliberately labour intensive, whereas the reverse is more usually the case, there being no point in making tropical agriculture (for example) more backbreaking than it already is. Technologies that are economically, socially and environmentally appropriate are so because they are financially profitable, socially rewarding and ecologically adaptive. Here the use of mechanically powered water pumps in place of ingeneous pedal driven devices is instructive. When a gallon of petrol will drive a motor and pump that lifts the same amount of water in twenty-four hours as eighteen men working three eight hour shifts, the weight of socially unrewarding and physical tedium this obviates is a technological improvement.[4] Replacing mechanical pumps with rustic animal driven devices may foster some notion of appropriateness in Northern eyes, but would fail to impress anybody in a poor country. Thus it would appear that in general it is an improvement to move away from labour intensiveness toward labour extensiveness, but only by starting from the bottom rather than in the middle of the labour spectrum.

Social acceptance and approval for a technology is vital, indeed it is usually more important in poor countries than prospects for economic gain through resource exploitation. Thus in striking a technological balance between monetary profit, social acceptability and environmental adaptability I defer first to social acceptability then to environmentally appropriate technology. Expressed differently, the claim can be made that technologies woven into society in a way which erode occupational castes are appropriate to a higher degree than technologies that are profitable and environmentally adaptive.

Another important aspect of the improving notion rests on appropriateness being accorded to technologies which resolve bottlenecks in production, and solve intractable problems. For example, a radio telephone system to supplement a postal service could cut delays in the delivery of perishable agricultural goods, yet rest technologically upon more, rather than less, sophistication.

Technological innovations which reduce extenal dependence, particularly for basic foodstuffs, oil and essential durables can add significantly to a feeling of national wellbeing. Self-sufficiency may be unattainable but self-reliance can be approached and is nationally improving even when a break in dependency results in some inefficiencies, lowered standards and higher costs. It also does much to guarantee political independence as well as adding to social satisfactions of a general kind.

Raising selected technology to a higher and more useful plane is, possibly, the most important improving notion of all. Putting an iron tip on wooden digging sticks, then later introducing iron headed tools, then moving to animal drawn implements—these are the step by step improvements that count. Technological jumps, such as moving from the personal messenger with a cleft stick to radio telephones can, of course, be worthwhile in some cases, but as a general rule, for the main occupational activities of agriculture and housebuilding, the social reinforcement that is so vital to success in technical reforms establishes the worth of moving step by step, consolidating each improvement before moving onto the next.

Problems of technological choice

That bundle of desirables—modernity, self-sufficiency and appropriateness—shows by seeming contradiction that making the right technological choice is no simple matter. It is self-evident that each time a choice has to be made these three ideals, plus all the factor proportions applicable at the time, have to be considered together. Clear cut answers are out of the question but some precepts can be derived.

One of these involves the already reviewed choice between socially rewarding and financially profitable alternative technologies. The clear general finding here is that distributive justice, as a widespread social reward, is more vital to the interests of low income countries than narrowly assessed improvements to the balance of payments. A specific objection arises when widespread social rewards derive from needlessly undignified backbreaking work dreamed up mainly to keep a population employed. Work for its own sake has no virtue; only the benefit derived from productive and creative effort fulfils that criterion.

A variation on the reward versus profitability theme is that which arises from having to choose between natural and synthetic technological alternatives. This is sometimes described as the choice between soft and hard technologies. Consider the case, described by Marsden, of the shoe making industry in a poor country where some 5,000 'soft' technology leather shoemakers are put out of work by the introduction of 'hard' technology plastic shoe moulding machinery using imported materials and operated by a handful of workers.[5] Were this nation in need of the skills for other more useful work, or were there a better external market for leather as a raw material, the case for hard (or synthetic) technology might be vindicated. This example shows that remaining with a soft (or natural) technology can sometimes prove appropriate for a nation in terms of balanced employment and resource use compatibility. In other words, the plea to retain soft technologies in circumstances such as that described by Marsden is not doctrinaire but is founded on logic—particularly economic logic. This single case study is just that, and would not necessarily prove to be universally applicable for natural technologies; but the general situation is that synthetic technologies require hard currency investment per workplace, employ few people of whom some are expatriate, and usually consume imported raw materials and export the profits or channel them to the already privileged in society.

Hard technologies can also produce synthetic toxins that are much more to be feared than biodegradable organic waste. Pollution of this kind, it must be noted, is more the problem of the wealthier nations where a correlation between production and environmental impact is apparent. Commoner and his associates show that the 'predominant factor in an industrial society's increased environmental degradation is neither population nor affluence, but the increasing environmental impact per unit of production due to technological changes'.[6] This assertion has, however, to be weighed up against other criteria before a universal ruling about technological change can be derived. A particularly Southern aspect of the argument is that waste is wrong and tantamount to an admission of defeat, whereas in the Northern nations the main concern is for environmental protection in itself. Technologies that produce organic and recyclable wastes cannot be faulted on that count alone, whereas technologies that produce deadly toxins and other synthetic compounds for disposal are to be feared; however, organic and consumer durable wastes are of lesser account in low income countries because they are largely recycled.

Technologies which produce toxins are usually introduced to poorer nations as exports from environmentally protectionist nations. In most low income countries scientific facilities are not up to the task of detecting the sophisticated outsider who may propose to can fish, manufacture plywood, produce fertilisers or refine a mineral ore; voiding waste from these projects, untreated, rendering the host country a pollution haven. The facilities of taxation and regulation, which were examined in the previous chapter, are available, but the poorer and less 'Northern' the economic structure of a low income economy, the more liable these facilities are to neglect and abuse. It can be easier, therefore, to control the technology at initial choice, as it were: yet this is a choice to be used reflectively. What is meant here is that organic and non-organic yet non-toxic pollution of dirtier but assimilable kinds can be tolerated and indeed welcomed. Examples include cement plants without precipitators at sites where windborne particulates are no threat to settled areas, fish canneries similarly sited, and tree milling and pulping projects located near river mouths. There will be environmental damage, but taken overall the employment and economic advantages often outweigh protectionist arguments. The technologies chosen in each case need not be bereft of controls, but the appropriateness of the technology chosen can vary from circumstance to circumstance and calls for flexibility and improvisation. Indeed, the very sophistication of pollution control technologies are such that industries can be started up at low production rates and with little pollution control with a view to applying limited low cost clean-up as production take off is reached, then applying more stringent and costly pollution controls when production is in full swing: depending, of course, on the industry and the specific processes involved.

Is 'smallness' in poor nations always so very 'beautiful'? Cities of over 100,000 lead to obvious practical diseconomies of food, water and raw materials supply; and the massive new dams of Africa, and now on the Indus, give rise to technical and environmental problems. Metropolitan centres with their universities, seats of government, commercial variety and artistic communities enshrine ideals as, indeed, can a monumental power dam, serving thereby to vindicate single centre metropolitanism to a limited extent. Other circumstances can arise where bigger is better; but small or big it is appropriateness, with economic as well as social and environmental overtones, which remains the overall criterion of selection. The pumping of ground water to the surface by means of tube wells affords an example. Should these wells be large facilities at ten mile centres owned and run by profiteers, or should they be smaller units (more costly to instal per unit of water raised) under local control? The lower construction and power supply costs for large units is only one side of a ledger which lends overwhelming social and technical support to the installation of numerous small units. The social costs of underemployment, together with the political price paid for placing control in the hands of others than those who consume the resource leads to the view that the matter of scale is one of 'conceiving grandly and acting discreetly'. This view, expressed in relation to tube well water supply, can also be extended to agriculture and industry generally. Bold plans, bound to stir people to action, should be backed up by technologically discreet, socially acceptable and economically modest implementation.

There is also a need to consider the scale of investment in terms of the capital cost for each workplace. External funding leading to multinational exploitation has been held (Chapter 4) to be unacceptable, not least in technological terms, but mainly because of the high cost per workplace. In poorer countries low cost workplaces cannot be created from internal revenues or by printing paper money so, perforce, a local yardstick has to be applied. Quarashi gives a capitalisation factor of 1.3 increasing to 6 to multiply against *per capita* national product.[7] Low capitalisation costs per workplace of this kind do, in general, result in a spreading out of environmental impact. This, as in the case of forests denuded to make charcoal for small industries, may be a disadvantage, and is a further point against limited scale technology. The well intended catch phrase, 'small is beautiful' is sincere, it is also one of the most fallacious foisted upon the arbiter of technological choice. Grand designs are simple yet massive; in order to be appropriate their implementation must be socially rewarding require modest capitalisation per workplace and replenish renewable resources. The scale of technologies chosen should be what they must 'appropriately' be, small or large.

Choosing between modern sophisticated technologies and time proven rustic practices is one of those 'either–or' issues, but the criteria for assessment are relatively clear. Apart from justifiable gain in the use of specific advanced technologies, such as in telecommunications, it can be adduced that sophistication equates with developmental and national frustration. This can be catalogued as arising from:[8]

1 Shortfalls in project attainment due to locally inadequate maintenance and repair services.

2 Disheartening returns resulting from unsound market research and investment advice.

3 Production or output problems due to management and personnel difficulties.

4 Conflict with an unsympathetic or confused civil service and local administration.

5 Breakdown of input infrastructure such as power and water supplies.

6 Disenchantment arising from the external payment of patent rights, the exporting of profits, expatriate personnel costs and money leaks.

7 Neglect of the rest of the economy, or the traditional sector being replaced by modern technology.

8 Increased unemployment and exacerbated underemployment.

Of course, the sophistication of technology is seldom a simple matter of deciding to manufacture or produce goods in a modern as opposed to a traditional way. Product characteristics—consider a tractor or motor car—impose technology with very little choice. Even basic agricultural implements, such as really good hand tools, cannot be beaten out by village blacksmiths; thus if a low income country takes a political decision to mass produce top quality hand tools they may have to do so under license and production control. A refined quality specification may dictate sophistication and this will, unintentionally, beget the eight complications just listed; the answer being to specify general performance criteria for technologies. This enables products to be made through locally available experience and know-how. Gradual changes to the product specification (such as fire proofing and safety in the case of housing) can introduce better techniques, and 'next step' improvements. Another example is the introduction of petrol driven pumps to replace human powered agricultural drudgery. With some sectors, such as communications, technological leaps might be contemplated to cut delays or to sweep inefficiency aside; but the best general approach is to seek the freeing of bottlenecks in basic life support activities (such as the examples in housing or agriculture just listed) through a gradualist policy attitude which aims to improve the next step.

Deciding between a technology offering a great deal of menial employment, and another which employs a skilled few is, aside from economic and environmental appropriateness, about the most important aspect of technological choice. Brick making illustrates the point. Across the northern part of the Indian sub-continent bricks are made by the time tested *bhatta* method. About two-thirds of the manual effort put into this labour intensive process (30 bricks per worker day) is absorbed in the drudgery of moulding clay, sand and water into wet bricks for sun drying. Children who should be at school, and women, are drawn into employment that, at best, can produce $15 per week for each household. Freed of the tedium of this labour the children could go to school, the women could care better for their young and the men could either work with technologically improved hand machinery or turn to housebuilding or agriculture. But the rub is, could they?

It is one thing to introduce labour saving, another to re-employ the labour so freed. The criterion is that undignified, poorly rewarded and socially unproductive labour is inappropriate, and if a technological way can be found to obviate it then that is social progress whether or not the ranks of the unemployed are increased. Thus in China the replacement during the time of Chairman Mao of human powered with mechanically driven agricultural pumps removed a production blockage (the need to shift large quantities of water quickly) thereby getting rid of a dehumanising practice; and in this way labour was also freed for more ingenious aspects of agriculture.[9] Technological improvements of this kind which undermine any employment caste system are worthy. Continuing up from the base toward extensiveness in employment offers other possibilities and complications. More explicitly, whereas the introduction of technological innovation to overcome degrading labour has just been expressed as an imperative, one has to be more cautious in considering the introduction of further technological innovations which reduce the employment of semi-skilled and artisan labour. My view here is that it is sound practice to move away from labour intensiveness, from the employment base up toward increasing labour extensiveness and efficiency in terms of output per worker, but only as is socially appropriate. Thus agriculturalists in densely settled countries would do as well to concentrate on improving their skills so that they gain more per unit of land, as well as more per unit of work. This reasoning would dignify semi-skilled labour by accommodating the granting of societal rewards for efficiency and ingenuity. A'from the base up'approach also avoids the need for retraining programmes and labour displacements and is, in this sense, both incremental and educational.

In so far as macro-policy is concerned, no nation can be wholly independent; but when technological policy and specific technological take up is being considered, a choice arises. It is not so much that technologies chosen from another nation are questionable. Far from it. What is open to doubt is the accompanying political dependency. Spreading out from the imported technology are tentacles such as hard currency loans, patent rights obligations, foreign manufacturing standards and the presence of expatriate personnel. Furthermore, the gains flowing back along these tentacles more often than not economically benefit the donor more than the recipient. Thus whilst technological independence is impossible, technological take up should be administered in such a way that the transfer can be run and maintained by local operators using the local material resources and be linked into allied industries and the domestic market. Widespread circulation of ideas about technological innovation is to be encouraged. In general it can be said that technological reforms which fulfil ecodevelopment criteria are more reliant upon the transfer of technological concepts between like-thinking nations than it is upon the North—South exchange of trinkets for raw materials.

Technological transfer

The importation of hardware under 'turn key' conditions has been described by Hayes as a situation where 'typically, the technology has worked, and the technology transfer has not'.[10] This is a problem which can be identified in the Middle East oil producing countries acquiring technological goods from industrialised nations. These are sometimes poor nations, yet they are hardly typical of the Southern world, nor do their peculiar factoral circumstances compel them to heed ecodevelopment ideals.

In the poorer, more typical, low income nations technological transfer consists in the main of introducing concepts into the information, administrative and political framework. With vertical technological transfer the transfer itself has, as it were, to work before the ʾrtefacts. The technological hardware involved is really secondary to the transfer of educational and administrative software. The amount of transformation that can be absorbed thereby becomes a constraining factor and may lead enlightened yet formerly backward economies to institute changes in educational policy as a prelude to enhancing long term receptivity. Of course, such countries will want technological changes which achieve production breakthroughs, but in the absence of newly found resource riches or heavy economic and political dependency the best procedure is to start from where matters stand, make incremental improvements, plug obvious technological gaps and cautiously test and take up new technologies for application to old retractable problems. Gradualism may induce some frustration, the control of which is a matter of social policy and political adroitness; but opponents to the concept should explain quite precisely just how else poorer people can gain higher living standards.

The transfer of technology for embodiment into the production and welfare parts of an economy takes place in several ways:

1 It is possible to identify communication links and information flows about new and improved technologies both abroad and within a nation; and here modern media facilities of the most sophisticated order (such as communications satellites) can be useful.

2 It is possible to acquire knowledge through the recruitment of outside advisors and the acquisition of patents.

3 Given political will and local receptivity, local technical and managerial training schemes can be mounted to educate and re-educate technologists and artisans.

4 Broad based education working from the bottom up can facilitate inquisitiveness about, inventiveness for and adaptability to new appropriate technologies.

5 Research centres and demonstration cells can be founded to study problems and disseminate findings.

6 Countries can enter agreements to share the results of collaboration; a particularly useful approach for major development projects such as damming a jointly owned river basin and for sophisticated technical problems such as transnational pollution.

To be adaptive and imitative in the selection of technology is, for any nation, a sign of their coming to terms with the principles of ecodevelopment.

Political feasibility and social acceptability is another dimension to technological transfer which must be examined. An important factor here is the maintenance of within-nation control over the means of production. This renders technological transfer more a political and social matter than an economic and technological issue. Here the tyranny of small thinking (such as labour intensive agriculture) is as much to be guarded against as excessive zeal for a 'wonder' project. The appropriate political stepping stones will include a concern for issues of importance to the political majority. Another would be to energise and extend existing linkages through communities, schools and workers' unions by encouraging them to study and take up technological transfers of economically, socially and environmentally compatible kinds. Another will be to alter regulations and to facilitate official changes of attitude to production and welfare policies. All these transfers to new, more appropriate, technologies and the revision of technological practices requires a commitment to technologically 'soft' policies.

Practical reforms

People are sustained by the natural resource endowment from which all food, energy, clothing and construction requirements are drawn. In this sense urbanisation is the technological manifestation which most seriously affects the natural environment. The deeper ramifications of urban focused technologies, with environmental consequences beyond the urban boundary, are serious. Marxist dogma falls short here because, although Marx saw no essential difference between agriculture and the urban milieu, both his admirers and detractors often chose to reflect a spirit of anti-ruralism which characterised agricultural workers as idiots.[11] Indeed, in both capitalist and socialist economies, the consequences of misunderstanding the relationship binding rural to urban life is reflected in the discharge of unwanted residuals and toxins into the atmosphere or the nearest water body. Thus the 'intermediate', 'appropriate', 'acceptable' or 'socially appropriate' technology movements about which so much that is thoughtful and useful is written are really very much of rural concern because they involve the majority of low income consumers and the majority manufacture of essential products for nutrition, shelter and clothing.

Technological inventiveness is, however, very much an urban and indeed a Northern nation urban phenomenon, even in its ultimate application to rural areas; and it is in the urban place that the more advanced energy saving and synthesising technologies can be applied. Sadly for the low income countries, this technological uplift from the Northern nations, and intended for them, is seen on the one hand as a patronising lower order of technology for rural areas and on the other as imitative technology intended for urban areas. In seeking rural or urban appropriate technologies the main difficulty is that of optimalising the capital, labour and resource utility mix in order to reduce the former, engage the penultimate and conserve the latter.

Energy generation, energy conservation and energy use—these are the matters which dominate technological reforms. Energy policy has to be based upon energy sources and resources. In some low income circumstances, fossil fuel and uranium deposits grant a lease to pursue 'hard' energy options. More often the 'softer' renewable sources, such as hydro potential and solar power have to be relied upon. This is to be preferred because, whilst low income countries are not running out of solar energy, they are depleting their fossil fuels. Of course, great amounts of these non-renewable fuels remain untapped, and their utilisation can bring short term and medium term benefits; but in general the hard energy route, particularly the nuclear option, will be denied the poorer nations because of an absence of the massive capital required to pay for imparted technologies of this kind. For poorer nations, already powered in the main from the solar source, the way forward is by means of improved soft energy policies involving further technological innovation. This is not only clear and imperative, it satisfies classical economic and Pareto-fulfilling criteria.

Technological reforms for rural application are somewhat facile, being mostly a matter of checking to see what 'next step' improvements ought to be contemplated. These next steps are frequently neglected because of governmental and local apathy. Important among them is rural electrification from hydro, solar and wind sources. The initial demand is not so much for massive supplies to power heavy machinery, as to let the day into the night, and to power radios and small electrically driven appliances that do so much to establish communication and to redress imbalances between rural and urban living. Low electrical energy requirements can be met cheaply from local sources; higher demand, requiring a national grid, can be very expensive and wasteful of what is in effect the most versatile form of energy. Biogas technology can be used to produce methane as a cooking fuel with high quality organic and mineral fertilisers as a by-product.[12] Windmill power can be used to lift water short heights, and in more isolated locations the use of diesel or petrol driven pumps is so mechanically efficient as to

172

vindicate their appropriateness. Other practical reforms in rural areas include the use of improved agricultural tools, the breeding of better draught animals, the sowing of higher yielding (if disease resistant) plant varieties, adoption of public health fundamentals and innovations to house design and construction. These are all significant. Of lesser importance, yet with a place, are such fringe 'cottage industry' activities as village soap, matches, paper, vegetable dehydration, weaving, grain milling and juice extracting industries. Couple some, a few, or many of these practical reforms to an organisational restructure and the quality of rural life and its comfort, convenience and pleasure can be vastly improved.

The concern with energy use in urban areas shifts attention away from the technological options already reviewed to matters of efficiency in its distribution and use. The practical reforms include a reduction in the energy embodied in the materials used and the techniques employed in the construction of buildings and infrastructure; and design improvements and shade tree planting that reduces inputs of energy absorbed to adjust (usually to cool down) working and domestic environments. Here it can be noted that vast amounts of low grade heat energy is dissipated by industry with little thought for the potential in these sources for domestic water heating and cooling. Further wasteful technologies of an industrial kind arise from the over packaging, over selling and erratic distribution of manufactured goods. Inefficiency is equally pronounced in intra-city movement, the practical reform most called for in this case being a reduction in the use of individual vehicles in favour of public transportation. All of these considerations have to be seen against the case made earlier for low capitalisation per workplace, with high but socially acceptable labour intensity and environmentally compatible technologies. These range across the panoply of manufacturing industries.

Industrial processing also involves recycling materials and extending the use of consumer durables. The case for material recycling is generally agreed and anyway, for low income nations, it is widely practiced. The extension of life for consumer durables raises the contention that poorer people have sometimes to make do with 'second best'. This argument is somewhat vacuous in that even British and American industries, for example, are known to have very old machinery and plant. Long life maintenance (already much practiced in the case of motor vehicles) and machinery brokerage services are called for. Finally, as was the case with rural reforms, managerial matters—organisational reforms in a sense— form a vital part of the endeavour to institute practical reforms of a technological kind. Understanding of and linkage into the production and marketing systems is important, as is a punitive price structure to attain energy consuming reforms.

Concluding comment

Two points I should like to make now are, firstly, that technology alone cannot materially advance a poor economy; and, secondly, that technological reform, like its namesake land reform, is as much a political as a practical matter. Thus 'appropriateness', in terms of technological endeavour, varies according to the satisfaction of people with their aims and the political interpretation and reaction to that satisfaction. From this simple analysis I have concluded that if one sees the main problem of a low income nation as that of simply increasing gross national product, the solution will be to engage in trade, maximise external borrowing and put a light hand on the economic regulator—but to expect no more than growth with distributional imbalances whereby the rich become proportionately fewer and disproportionately richer whilst the poor become relatively poorer and more numerous. However, if one sees the main need of such a nation as that of attaining overall progress, one will be drawn to examine the political paths which seek out the implementation of technological reforms.

What are these political paths? I believe that in the main they arise in poor countries from the left—what other power have the poor majority than their votes, and could it ever be conceived that they would use that power to highlight a polarity which makes the rich richer, leaving them where they are?—it being impossible to imagine the poor poorer! Education and the communication of information are other powerful levers. It may be that present generations will not witness much of a move toward economic self-reliance, social harmony and environmental equilibrium, but the generations which follow can be better educated and informed, and it becomes a moral—political responsibility to see that this becomes so.

The Northern nation industrial revolution gave rise to their successes and problems, and technological reform in the low income nations today has very little in common with that phenomenon. The market potential the Northern nations faced 150 years ago does not arise today; technology is sophisticated now; and the capitalist prediliction is being substantially eroded. Technological reform is one thread to a resolution of problems for the low incomed, on their own terms, because it satisfies economic, social and environmental criteria. This will often mean that a technically inferior project or process will be adopted because of the high employment it retains, the resources it conserves or the economic distribution it sustains, which is precisely how ecodevelopment equates with progress.

Notes

1   Maurice F. Strong, 'Progress or Catastrophe: Wither Our World?', *Environmental Conservation*, vol.2, no.2, Foundation for Environmental Conservation, Lausanne, 1975.

2   Ansel Adams and Nancy Newhall, *This is the American Earth*, Sierra Club, San Francisco, 1964, p.88.

3   M.M. Qurashi, *The Appropriateness of Technology Transferred*, Appropriate Technology Development Organisation, 1978 (mimeographed).

4   Hayes claims that 'At current US prices, 2.5¢ worth of gasoline can perform as much work as a healthy adult labouring from dawn to dusk'. Denis Hayes, *Energy for Development: Third World Options*, Worldwatch Paper 15, Worldwatch Institute, Washington, 1977, p.9.

5   K. Marsden, 'Progressive Technologies for Developing Countries', *International Labour Review*, vol.101, 1970, p.475.

6   Barry Commoner, Michael Corr and Paul J. Stamler, 'The Causes of Pollution', *Environment*, vol.13, no.3, p.19.

7   Qurashi, op.cit., p.9.

8   C.C. Onyemelukwe, *Economic Underdevelopment: An Inside View*, Longmans, London, 1974, p.16.

9   The Chinese have, rather interestingly, kept their large projects labour intensive to a technological fault. One can presume that as tens of thousands of workers are brought to these projects the opportunity is taken to lend solidarity to their beliefs and link that process to participation in the construction of monumental public works?

10   Hayes, op.cit., p.11.

11   As, for example, by Colin Fry in 'Marxism Versus Ecology', *The Ecologist*, vol.6, no.9, November 1976.

12   In May 1977 the China News Agency reported that 100,000 technicians had constructed 4.3 million operational biogas plants.

9 Some operational tactics

> The object is to point out the dangers of imprudence
> and the necessity of caution in all operations which
> interfere with the spontaneous arrangements of the
> organic world.
>
> *George P. Marsh* 1864[1]

It has been suggested in earlier chapters that the new direction of eco-development serves largely to displace a preoccupation with the rate of economic growth. What must now be offered to poorer nations is the more certain promise of improved average material lifestyles. The case for ecodevelopment rests on improved survival through the balanced use of resources. Getting to this state of balance can be identified as the main practical or operational problem.

Low income countries do need growth when it can be attained. For most nations this involves bringing in previously untapped resources from 'new frontiers', mainly the oceans and savannahs, through exploitation; plus production improvements, particularly in agriculture. Administrative practicality has to be bound together with these policies. It is here that political figures emerge as touchstones, while the more deliberative administrative cadres, provided they can be persuaded to accept ecodevelopment, are the power behind the political throne. A difficulty is that senior administrators are so frequently appointed at the pleasure of, and are thus remunerated through, the political system. Their resistance to policy change is inertial. Take, for example, the call self-sufficiency makes to reject external aid. Who benefits more from aid than bureaucrats? None would suffer most from its denial than the same group. It is in this way that the relationship between these political nodes and the planning network, two important subjects in this chapter, can be seen to be vital.

Where majority political support for ecodevelopment exists then the mechanics whereby political figures activate the planning network will, a few hiccups excepted, work adequately enough. Centralised direction has its inefficiencies, but given conviction at the policy taking level it can subvert resource depletion or pollution hazards by decree.

Ecodevelopment arises from the fusion of political economy and political ecology. Doom if 'we' or 'they' do not do something is a frequent prediction. But who are the 'we' and how can 'they' articulate concern as action? The owners of real estate and industrialists might be indicted here, but with the exception of their concern to keep domestic and recreational environments aesthetically pleasing, they are little worried about other effects external to them. Local and central government administrations are beholden to their political masters. When the call 'they ought to do something' goes up in response to a resource ravaging or polluting circumstance, citizens feel as ineffective as in most Northern nations, which leaves environmental protection to the tender vagaries of the laws of nuisance. Local and central government can make little effective response to pleas for better schools, drains and water supplies, let alone take on the big business polluter or resource exploiter. 'We' can also mean the public at large, represented in poor countries by the average impecunious, underfed, apprehensive individual. But give that mass of population an understanding of the equality latent in ecodevelopment policy and a strong political force is brought into focus. In this way an ethos can be identified for ecodevelopment; but a more important locus is the conscience of individuals, particularly political individuals. My advocacy is to elect responsible and truly representative leaders who will (preferably through democratic procedures rather than by 'agreement') particularly espouse the cause of the rural poor. They cannot then overlook ecodevelopment policies.

Theoretically, environmental imperatives are politically neutral, but in practice there are recognisable right and left alliances to resource conservation, pollution control and environmental preservation. Here Stretton is uncompromising:

> To build better equalities into programmes of environmental reform, the only imaginable equalisers are the political parties of the Left . . . [and] they must try to attract diverse support not so much by abandoning class politics as by diffusing egalitarian values into policy, offering equitable environmental action, equitable housing and urban policies and fairer distributions of wealth and income.[2]

He writes, it should be explained, for the advanced countries; the world's poor has no appreciable environmental press. I align with the environmental standpoint, but I remain detached from the political sentiment because of the propensity for the political left to be effective in resource conservation and distribution and for the political right to be effective with environmental preservation of aesthetic kinds. These strengths and weaknesses are useful or a hindrance depending upon circumstances.

Planning networks

Planned decision taking is, simply, forethought before causative action. The forethought may arise in the realm of market choice where people make their own relatively random decisions in ways familiar to all of us as individuals; or in the realm of political discretion where representatives make decisions supposedly on behalf of a community but often for their own aggrandisement. The content of decision taking is in three parts, not necessarily divided and separated. There is the problem solving context whereby a material or human function is assessed and a correction path proposed; there is the potential realising context whereby an assessment is made of human expectations relative to resource availability and a development goal is proposed; and there is the regulative context whereby agreed behaviour norms are enforced. The process of decision making, which is a sequential matter, involves:

1 Emergence of the awareness of the need or desire for planning, policy making or decision taking.
2 Formulation of objectives.
3 Obtaining agreement to proceed.
4 Assembling a planning agency, assigning responsibilities and outlining a procedure.
5 Assembling and evaluating data.
6 Deriving plan goals and the formulation of a tentative plan.
7 Testing of the tentative plan and its programme.
8 Statement of targets, and the formulation of a more final plan and a programme.
9 Testing the more final plan and its programme—this time involving the public.
10 Gaining approval.
11 Implementation.
12 Completion or review.

The lineality shown here is only true in the most simple examples for there is always some looping and relooping. Furthermore, the move from stage 5 to stage 6 usually gives rise to a number of alternative possibilities.

Decision taking, plan making and policy formulation are all character-ised by forethought. This leads to choosing a preferred strategy, usually a compromise between the best technical solution and the means avail-able for effecting it. Were there just these two variables, something near the correct mix between technical excellence and the power to deliver results might be attained; but uncertainties of other kinds arise. Paucity or inaccuracy of data may lead to social and environmental consequences of unpredictable kinds; a lack of shared understanding and co-ordination between governmental and institutional sectors may lead to duplication of effort or the overuse of resources; misinterpreted political values may lead to a shortfall in community aspirations.

Environmental planners are custodians of some of society's values; political figures are custodians of others more broadly significant; and individuals of others particularly important to themselves. Getting these three perspectives clear lies at the heart of effective planning—a design activity because it involves forethought. On the one hand it is logical, predictive and deterministic and on the other intuitive, imaginative and probalistic. It is impossible, given the three masters to be served (plan-ners, politicians and the public) to get it absolutely right. When data imperfections, personnel shortages and economic stringencies abound, as is almost always the case, then a comprehensive approach has to be thrown over in favour of a selective strategy which links projects and policy. This activity undertaken in the shadow of a grand design, would be one way to depict the operational mechanics involved.

One enormous difficulty for the planners is that of applying essenti-ally simple concepts to improve upon an infinitely complex world. Given all the data, all the personnel and all the resources desired, the planner could, theoretically, arrive at a full set of problem solving and potential realising recommendations. But such ideal operational situa-tions seldom arise. Thus planners are obliged to show a flexibility to learn and re-learn through feedback from participation and statistical measurements of successes and mistakes so that reappraisal leads to improvement.

The planning apparatus

Much of the routine regional, rural and urban planning effort can be, unflatteringly, described as planning to reinforce the *status quo*. Plan-ning for ecodevelopment has a watchdog component, but in essence it strives to reflect some new ideals, the motivating source for planning.

As with any other relatively new process, there is an interim stage when credibility has to be established. In this period goals have to be

180

met in an atmosphere of data uncertainty, even if the overall objectives are clear. In addition, there are problems with the training and recruitment of personnel. Two clear strictures are, firstly, not to allow the formulation of objectives to become constipated by data demands (which is not the same as decision taking without full consideration of the facts); and, secondly, to work selectively in the shadow of the grand design referred to earlier as ecodevelopment.

Data problems include delays in data handling as well as data assembly, and can severely hamper any new endeavour. The factual data assembly and diagnostic rules are clear: the data gathered needs to be of a kind that is *suitable* in that it is adequate for the uses to which it is to be put; reflects *economy* in that it is gathered at a cost that can be afforded; and that it is gathered with *efficiency* so that delays are avoided. These three strictures are straightforward and easily agreed. What often happens though is that data assembly and diagnosis dominates, whereas planning is of course concerned with development, not the production of data or analyses. This in turn means that if there is a disinclination to plan in accordance with ecodevelopment principles then it may be that the planning guidelines are not well enough understood, indicating that these, as a first step, must be clearly established.

Getting on with plan making is only one of the interim difficulties. Another is to establish operational credibility for ecodevelopment where little exists. A ploy worth adopting here is to glean the existing laws, statutory orders and ministerial directives of governmental, commissioned and institutional bodies, and to collate all the administrative functions and activities relating to ecodevelopment. A summary of these existing powers, published as guidelines, would establish a wide range of latent powers that can be enlisted. Getting these ecodevelopment guidelines translated into policies and projects raises the problem of the role of already established sub-national planning agencies, for it will prove more efficacious to link into them than to make an attempt to dominate them. They are embedded within the command, financing and information systems and they are already well established. With regional, rural and urban planning agencies (given political support) ecodevelopment can get ahead; without this it will wither.

Problem solving and potential realising activities are both part of policy forming and plan making. Finding solutions involves first identifying the problems and then commending the optimum benefit solution. Thus 'problems' can be largely 'solved' by servo-mechanical methods which involve diagnosis followed by corrective treatment. Putting up potential realising scenarios for alternative futures is a more complicated matter because with this approach answers cannot be attained, only approached. Intuition, imagination and a flexible attitude are called for. The alternative future has to be planned from little or nothing. Sub-national planners embroiled in the toils of regulative controls often lack the necessary overall perspective to perform well in this way.

How, in potential realising situations, to proceed strategically is a matter of principle; how to proceed operationally is a matter of technique. Once the call for the adoption of ecodevelopment policy has been made at political and central administrative levels the temptation to apply these guidelines in all sub-national planning enterprises arises; but initially there is no way by which data, personnel or funds will be adequate. What can, and has to be done, is to work piecemeal project-by-project in accordance with the guidelines for ecodevelopment—the understanding being that success will gain recognition and breed further success through the grasp it makes first on ideals and then on the data, personnel and cash flows it triggers off.

The regulative apparatus

Planning agencies draw up problem solving and potential realising policies, plans and projects, and regulate changes in land occupancy and land use. This latter control activity is, it can be argued, more important than futuristic scenario writing. So it is, if the guidelines for ecodevelopment are right; the reason being that effective policy is of more utility than a beautiful yet impractical plan. Furthermore, while most planning has to score, project by project, success hopefully multiplying success, it leaves in its wake a host of problems that violate the tenets of ecodevelopment. Control is the administrative filling between spatially separated projects in that it can be applied on a comprehensive basis, continuously. In general, the main concern is for the *occupancy* matters of land using, density of land occupation and access. In an ecodevelopment context the emphasis will lie more on *performance* matters such as the fulfilment of health, safety and energy criteria together with the utilisation of socially appropriate technology and the generation of employment. Occupancy and performance strictures have always been identifiable in conventional planning models; ecodevelopment merely refocuses this practice to performance criteria. Twin difficulties besetting ecodevelopment control are firstly that overzealous efforts may induce the more footloose developer to go elsewhere; second there is the operational problem of instilling into this service an understanding of ecodevelopment principles.

Operational management

The interface between new policy and the already established administrative machinery presents complications. This is equally the case at local levels of acceptability, it being one serious problem to align central policy to ecodevelopment, and quite another matter to get local government functionaries to appreciate and act for the same cause.

Another management item is uncertainty of outcome. Development policy focussed unblinkingly upon production has one clear goal—profit. Ecodevelopment policy shows a concern for some measurables, such as the distribution of goods, but also for other matters such as resource conservation, environmental protection and pollution abatement, which are difficult to quantify. It is for this reason that the expression 'environmental management' is set aside in favour of ecodevelopment—development of conventional kinds (if that is attainable) plus a component of concern for environmental virtues.

In already overdeveloped nations the rustic component within ecodevelopment upholds in that circumstance the case for decentralisation. In low income countries this is impractical because, desirable though small government may seem, ecodevelopment guidelines can really only be disseminated from the top down. This can initiate one or a combination of results.

1 An increase in staff in one central ministry or new environmental protection agency brought into being to uphold a concern for environmental protection and resource conservation.

2 The creation of a variety of specialist sub-agencies to handle other aspects of environmental policy (e.g. national parks, tourism, large resource exploitation projects).

3 The delegation and passing on of ecodevelopment responsibilities to other government departments (such as health and industry) and to local government.

Fragmented responsibility perpetrates a confusion that has to be guarded against, yet, given recognisably effective support for ecodevelopment, the establishment of these three outgrowths are vindicated because it is mainly by inter-agency linkages formed on the basis of co-operation rather than competition that ecodevelopment can flourish. The central foci would, in terms of management, be concerned with the following:

1 *Detection:* the recording and collation of environmental, social and economic data changes, together with sensitivity analysis relating to those changes.

2 *Information:* the provision, on a service basis, of codes of ecodevelopment conduct and interpretations of policy to all agencies of local and central government.

3 *Fiat:* the publicising of powers of an environmental kind that are already available, together with the preparation of new legislative and regulative powers.

4 *Implementation:* the technical, political and administrative linkages to production and welfare for the mobilisation of policy.

Management studies may appear far removed from ecodevelopment; and in the sense that this subject area is a separate science no attempt need be made here to reiterate its specifics.[3] Nevertheless, some cautionary items should be stressed. A first is that the rights and values of minority communities are humanly precious and essential to the integrity of modern nations. A second is that widespread information sharing and publicity is the only way to have ecodevelopment policies understood and agreed. A third is the need for institutional adaptability so that policies and agencies can be readily changed to accord with new conditions and requirements as ecodevelopment policies evolve and strengthen. A fourth is to involve all agencies of local and central government, indeed all significant parties and institutions, in the preparation of proposals and the taking of decisions.

Large projects

Whilst ecodevelopment is for growth wherever this is attainable, it can be seen that in terms of scale, big projects are in many ways at odds with ecodevelopment ideals. This is so because they embrace large investments of external capital, require imported technology and employ expatriate personnel. Nevertheless, the economic growth component of composite ecodevelopment does not rule out large scale proposals. These may be of a 'policy' character such as tourist expansion, or take a 'project' form, such as a large dam or a mining enterprise. The essential primary strategy is to consider the environmental, social and economic issues together at the concept stage when the political decision about such proposals is taken.

What also has to be considered carefully by decision takers are the distinctive entrepreneurial, power bloc and community elements of involvement and concern. The expatriate entrepreneur participates solely to make a substantial risk-covering profit from minimum proportions of investment. Other governments or power blocs, if not involved for profit, are present to serve their political objectives. The community wherein a massive proposal is situated also seeks monetary profit, but in addition it would like to have unemployment reduced, traditional virtues respected, local production enhanced and acquire an expansion in technical expertise. This is the complex character of the balance between entrepreneurial, external and community interests that has to be weighed up and struck; and in that weighing up it is important to recall that as big projects unfold toward culmination (or maximum output) the diseconomies of environmental and social kinds tend to increase. In other words, tourism at its seasonal peak, a mine at optimum production and a new highway at completion all contribute, at that time, to maximum environmental degradation and cultural shock. Governments should foresee the consequences emanating from major projects in this way because, from the perspective of the expatriate entrepreneur or external foreign power, the first objective is to get a foot in the door, leaving such problems as unforeseen social disruption or pollution to be attended to later when and if public outcry calls for corrective action.

One fear harboured by decision takers is that, should they set down strictures of an environmental kind, these alone may cause the entrepreneurs to move to politically less constrained climates. Big project financiers know their arithmetic, and usually they are much more clearly aware of the likely profits than the governments with whom they deal. But whereas they are thinking in terms of a 100 or 200 per cent return on investment 'the additional cost attributed to the environmental and health safeguards incorporated into projects has ranged from zero to three per cent of the total project cost'.[4] These proportions must be kept in mind in order to ensure that entrepreneurial bluff is understood for what it represents; the ultimate profit squeeze; seeking to commit governments to the acceptance of proposals they would normally wish to defer, consider more deeply, amend or reject.

Huge dams and state farms are as much characterised locally by failure as success,[5] calling not so much for outright early rejection but proven technical understanding before decisions are reached—for the simple reason that failure has a social as well as an economic cost. A further consequence to consider is that even big, successful proposals leave large numbers of people and vast regions of territory unbenefitted, as can best be observed in relation to the 'windfalls' of tourism which fall unevenly, and the odd agricultural pilot project which leaves local farmers little better off and may indeed exacerbate their problems. A final complication that can be noted is that the very purposefulness of big proposals, which may articulate other activities and jobs, should lead governments to consider whether this is going to overburden their capacity to provide accessory welfare and communications services.

What is clear in relation to big projects is:

1 That governments must consider all financially, environmentally and socially insignificant projects at the highest level of government, it being the cabinet's burden of responsibility to decide what is or is not significant.

2 That negotiations about major projects and proposals should be moved forward cautiously at the initial stages.

3 That project packages must articulate Economics (including energy economics), Equity (social balance), Engineering (design) and the Environment (resource conservation and amenity protection); in all the four big E's, together as equals at the design stage and during implementation—the 'Equartet'.

Agricultural and forestry proposals

These contain separate policy and project distinctions. For example, agreement to accept the use of higher yielding grain varieties might be thrust forward as agricultural policy. Given caution and forethought it should be possible to spread the obvious benefits widely and to safeguard the economic interests of those who hold land suitable for this scale of agricultural enterprise. The large scale agricultural project such as plantation, or animal ranching, is operationally akin to an industrial process where the difficulty is one of seeing that the propensity to consume power and other resources does not overstrain production capacity or run ahead of the ability of the market to absorb its products. With agricultural and forestry policies and projects the valuable, virtually irreplaceable resources, are viewed by the developer as raw materials for exploitation; whereas governments have a responsibility to ensure the continued regeneration of soils and the rehabilitation of forests.

Mining proposals

Major mining proposals are exploitative and invoke single purpose investments in access roads, mine site settlement, power generation and transmission, disposal of overburden, restoration of tailings and mineral milling. Sometimes, as in the case of oil exploitation, the 'one off' income being derived represents the main underpinning of the local economy for the rest of its human history. But although this local interest is clear, it frequently becomes crushed between the entrepreneurial and governmental millstones.

Mining management is always far more 'efficient' than government monitoring and accounting. Downstream and downwind pollution abatement will, if at all possible, be overlooked by mining managements. Apart from striking the right apportionment of dividends, this is the major practical problem. Community displacement and social disorder represent another price to pay. An agreed government position on levies and taxes, plus co-operation in land acquisition, can induce mining companies to co-operate in the provision of health and training facilities, and to assist with the monitoring of waste disposal. Despite this, what has to be kept in perspective is that altruism and mineral exploitation do not equate: mining in low income countries is for money, and it is only because of relatively short term assured profits that mining organisations will give technical assistance, such as the monitoring of pollution which most governments are unable to provide on their own account. For the really massive mining enterprises, from which governments may garner considerable financial gain, the need will arise for official control expertise to be appointed, at a cost usually equal to less than 1 per cent of gains, in order to measure and report upon overburden disposal and the dispersal of toxic wastes.

Massive power producing projects

These implicate some of the better off (intermediate) nations in energy conversion of a nuclear order, which introduces ultimate dangers, for it is not possible to site a reactor or a processing plant anywhere in the world and guarantee its freedom from accident, riots or guerrilla activity. In other words, absolute political stability (which exists nowhere) is called for in order to house the most diabolical process mankind has ever fabricated. Nuclear power production is therefore untenable. That previous costings of 'safe' installations are proving to be prohibitive gratifies that contention; and that poorer nations may not be able to afford nuclear power, thereby taking them out of the nuclear target zone, makes them that much better off. By the year 2000 solar energy along with the use of coal will again be supreme and that, at least, will be to the advantage of low income nations.

A further complication for all power producing projects is that of low grade thermal waste disposal, usually through the use of cooling water which, particularly in tropical environments, leads quickly to ecological imbalance. Then there is solid waste disposal which—in the case of fuel ash—is of manageable proportions but which—in the case of nuclear solids—raises difficult technical problems. Hydro-power generation is the least polluting but the most geographically limiting form of power production; but if the geographical isolation of huge hydro schemes from urban areas is seen as a disadvantage, the longer term potential of small scale rural schemes can be seen as a positive advantage. The disruptive effects of large hydro dams requires that upstream flooding and downstream interruptions to flow are fully considered when the project decision is taken. These considerations are frequently overlooked at the costing and design stage.

Public utility and industrial projects

These vary greatly in their funding base, but both call for similar strictures in terms of environmental protection. In the private sector, governments (especially authoritarian governments) can enforce the polluter-pays-principle; but for their own public utility projects they are prone to overlook its application. With public utility and industrial schemes, pollution tends to be more easily controlled when projects are small and employ locally available resources and socially acceptable technologies. Agreement about small scale and low disturbance thresholds, together with a publicity programme about private and public responsibility, are components of greater importance than fine standards of chemical and particulate pollution. Not all the disadvantages are so tangible. The payment of minimum wages, employment of child labour, royalty non-payment for the use of resources, consumer discharge violations, consumer tax avoidance and dispersal neglect form a sorry list of external diseconomies which can, overall, render an otherwise economically attractive project socially unacceptable and environmentally repugnant.

Open water exploitation

Exploitation, particularly of the oceans, is more a matter of policy enforcement than project control. New international treaties could bring 35 per cent of the oceans under sovereignty. Where fishing is important to an economy then an institutional capacity must be built up to enforce principles of husbandry which will ensure stock regeneration. With exploitation of the seabed the main problem which arises falls under equity, the matter of dividing gains justly. Enforcement of regulations that will inhibit the generation of pollution together with contingency funding for abatement and compensation in the event of spillage are also important.

Tourism

Tourism equally involves policy enforcement and project control. Much profit can be made from tourism; but a great deal of unintended environmental and social change can follow in its wake. The important central element in tourist policy is for a nation to have tourism on their own terms and for their own direct benefit. A country that can largely own and manage tourism as an industry, provide transportation and control the issue of entry permits, is going a long way to maximising public benefits whilst safeguarding environmental and cultural values. The governments of many small nations have, however, allowed their territories to become soft option havens for tourism from which they gain little more than the hiring out of servant labour.

Natural and human disasters

Disasters generate special, random and unpredictably massive 'projects'. They often open up abnormal flows of assistance which can seriously disrupt the normal economy of a whole country. Food as aid can particularly undermine the food producing and distribution system, and should be accepted with strict cautionary controls. Equally important are post-disaster projects designed to get life back to normal, and to improve upon that norm through massive engineering works. These may be portrayed as humanitarian responses, but there is usually a minimising or misunderstanding of the human circumstances which contribute to a disaster. The guiding principle to apply in a post-disaster situation is first to supply humanitarian aid, then bring about a reversal of the administrative policies and social practices which induced or abetted the disaster. In an overpopulated savannah under drought this may mean human or animal depopulation; in a hurricane area rebuilding with wind-proof structures; in an earthquake zone out migration or the reconstruction of quake resistant low rise dwellings; and in areas liable to flood early warning systems and evacuation programmes coupled to waterway realignment. There is always a contributing element of human ineptitude to identify in the post-event analysis of 'natural' disasters, and that these are identified and rectified is as much a priority as immediate relief.

Nothing has been stated, so far, about environmental impact assessment (EIA) and energy accounting. In the case of EIA there is widespread dissatisfaction with the working of the procedure, coupled to the fact that it more often leads directly to legal profiteering than to environmental safeguards.[6] Energy accounting is also, as yet, underdeveloped.[7]

The EIA procedure is seldom invoked on environmental grounds alone because there are other social and economic factors to consider. The usual EIA preoccupation is the assessment of aesthetic and protectionist values. The lower priority is human health and nutrition—the ecodevelopment perspective. Top priority goes to economic assessment of losses and profits. These priorities should be switched. The EIA procedure does have a useful application for big proposals of publicly and privately financed kinds. A four point procedured breakdown for an EIA, whether submitted voluntarily or upon government request, runs:

1 Preparation by the proposed developer of an environmental impact statement. Here governments should make it clear that such statements must not be public relation sops, but be actually useful and intelligible. (Guidelines may be given to the developer. When a review of a preliminary statement has been submitted and shown to be inadequate, it should be referred straight back.)

2 On receipt of an adequate statement, arrangements would be made to publicise (over, say, 100 days) its content and general availability to all concerned, with an invitation to send in comments, to be collated as submissions.

3 Copies of the collated submissions would be referred back to the developer for the appendage of counter comments.

4 The environmental impact statement, the submissions (together with the counter comments) are then to be placed in the hands of a commission or tribunal for environmental audit. The commission's recommendations would be advisory in character and would lie with government to enforce as it sees fit.

189

Environmental impact assessment in the past has often been little more than design and environmental cosmetics—in effect a clean up proposal after the investment decision has been taken. To work well it must therefore be engaged as an equal input to the 'E quartet'—economics, equity, engineering and environment—and it must be conducted in an open way because of the complex social, economic and environmental criteria involved. Matthews holds the view that, 'The analyst need not be absolutely correct in choosing his criteria (in fact he never could be); but he must be explicit'.[8] But for organisational difficulties, the EIA procedural device could lead to negotiated agreements of 'best fit' solutions.

With energy accounting, the aim is not so much to pursue the energy paths within a project, and to account for them, as to establish a design criterion additional to economic assessment. Clearly projects such as a state farm, or a highway, can be designed in many different ways. There can be a 'hard' high energy sophisticated approach at one end of the design spectrum (using a great deal of foreign capital, expatriate personnel and imported components) and there can be a locally devised 'soft' low energy rustic approach at the other end. Which design a low income country might choose is a function of locally obtainable fuels, the labour unemployed at the time, power bloc pressures, political expediency and local urgencies. Energy accounting, again employed at the 'E quartet' stage, can serve usefully to arrive at a financially, socially and technologically appropriate project design. In the case of an energy producing project, such as a hydro electric dam, the energy return over the planned life of the installation can discount negatively. The embodied energy outlay for initial construction is a proportion of the ultimate energy gain. It is in this same way that construction energy values for non-breeder nuclear plants, which are about 2—5 per cent of ultimate energy output, can be produced to show how 'cheap' they are; the catch being that winning, processing, running and disposing of the waste from a plant using uranium ore sources below .002 per cent in grade can ultimately, and ironically, absorb more energy than is produced. There are not, it need hardly be added, vast quantities of high grade uranium ore.

Concluding comment

This review of operational strategies indicates the main elements of practice which underpin ecodevelopment policy. Practical planning is a technical process within which social objectives, environmental resources and economic realities form the major determinants. Thus it could be observed in review that the social connotation conveyed by reference to security, fairness and justice, the physical connotation carried forward by references to resource conservation, and the aesthetic connotation carried forward by references to environmental protection, can all broadly be interpreted in policy terms as attempting social and economic optimalisation through ecodevelopment. National and sub-national planners are in a delicate and often difficult position in relation to the spatial and organisational elements within this matrix. Horizontally, as it were, they are expected to have a broader than local vision, while vertically their work is expected to span a number of organisational boundaries. Lifting the horizon of political and administrative conscience to embrace ecodevelopment principles calls for relatively enormous adjustments. Paucity of aid establishes that there is no 'free lunch', and there are very few technological fixes; yet a much improved average life is there for poorer people in low income nations to take up through ecodevelopment.

Notes

1   G.P. Marsh, *Man and Nature: Physical Geography as Modified by Human Action,* 1864. Reprinted, D. Lowenthal (ed) Belknap Press, Harvard, 1965.

2   Hugh Stretton, *Capitalism Socialism and the Environment,* Cambridge University Press, Cambridge, 1976, p.13.

3   Stahrl Edmunds and John Letey, *Environmental Administration,* McGraw-Hill, New York, 1973. A useful reference text.

4   World Bank Group, *Environment and Development,* World Bank, Washington, 1975, p.3.

5   For example, the upstream and downstream effects of the Akosombo dam project in Ghana detailed by David Hart in 'The Volta River Project' unpublished doctoral study, University of Edinburgh, 1977; also the much studied post-World War II 'Ground Nut' scheme in East Africa.

6   For a useful critique, see Department of Architecture, University of Illinois, Symposium Proceedings, *Environmental Impact Analysis,* University of Illinois, Urbana, 1976.

7   Research studies in energy accounting are being undertaken by J.R. Coyne in association with the author at the Department of Land Economy, University of Cambridge.

8   William H. Matthews, 'Objective and Subjective Judgements in Environmental Impact Analysis', *Environmental Conservation,* vol.2, no.2, Foundation for Environmental Conservation, Lausanne, Summer 1975.

PART IV

OVERVIEW

10 Reshaping internal order

> Given the abandonment of the ideology of growth,
> the redirection of technological effort becomes
> possible and its contribution to a harmonious relation
> of man and nature immense.
>
> *I.G. Simmons, 1974*[1]

The dictum, that you cannot have your cake and eat it, is apposite. We can either pace our consumption of a resource keeping some in reserve or, if we are greedy or under competitive pressure, use it up as voraciously as possible. This latter incentive lies particularly with the major resource consumers in the already overdeveloped Northern nations, despite an objective wisdom which would advocate consumption, particularly energy consumption, at a rate of need rather than in terms of material desires.

These rich Northern nations suffer from other problems, however, such as twenty million nutritionally deficient in the USA, massive rates of mental ill health in Sweden, acute disorganisation in Italy, unemployment in Britain and France and constraints upon movement in Eastern Europe. These problems arise directly or as side products of affluence and indicate dangers and uncertainties no poor nation would want. Another matter to reflect upon is that the poorer low income nations have values and lifestyles that are, in many respects, the envy of rich nations, where every muscle and nerve is strained to secure facilities for leisure-taking only for it to transpire that there is no time left to savour that enjoyment. This gets us back to fundamentals; human progress derived from the land, and in particular material improvements founded upon resources of a renewable kind which are the basis of human survival. The practical limits to the extraction of some vital non-renewable resources are now in sight.

Policy in command

A 'policy core' was the first item in the eleven point listing of ecodevelopment principles given in Chapter 1. The full list ran:

1 Establish an ideological commitment.
2 Sharpen political and administrative integrity.
3 Attain international parity.
4 Alleviate poverty hunger.
5 Eradicate disease misery.
6 Reduce arms.
7 Work closer to self-sufficiency.
8 Clean up urban squalor.
9 Balance human numbers with resources.
10 Conserve resources.
11 Protect the environment.

The absence of an economic centrepiece to this listing underscores my conclusion that human advance for the impoverished and downtrodden in low income countries cannot be approached solely from an econometric standpoint. An alternative to Northern nation models and modelling has been advanced, the overall aim being to examine a way by which low income nations can overcome the weary growth rhetoric. Thus, instead of economic growth as an end in itself, I would assert that alleviating hunger and disease, reducing expenditure on arms, and the rest of the eleven factor specific policies should dominate; and that economic planning of Northern capitalist and communist kinds be accorded a subservient role in the future. This somewhat uncompromising statement is, hopefully, more enlightened than Draconian in that it is directed towards improving the plight of those disadvantages from birth through caste, serfdom, class or gender by increasing opportunities for individual fulfilment, household self-sufficiency and community self-reliance—the theme arising from Chapter 4.

The life support guidelines discussed in Chapter 5 lent organisational emphasis to the earlier eleven point policy listing, but again without an economic predominance. Stress was laid upon organisation and linkages. Subsequent chapters (6 to 9) were factor specific in that they set down some guidelines for resource utilisation and population limitation, economic programming, technological reform and, finally, operational strategies. However, in all this the relationship of ecodevelopment to power is centrally important if any change is to occur and therefore we must turn briefly to it.

> Power is a multi-dimensional concept and consists of different components... Firstly, there is physical violence such as used by armies, police forces, and informal groups or even individual political extremists and terrorists. The second and third components are of an economic character: power deriving from coalitions and monopoloid organisations; and power deriving from the possession of scarce resources, whether natural resources or human qualities (intelligence, leadership or personal attractiveness). A fourth is the power of custom or law, sometimes recognised as a legal basis for certain types of behaviour. The fifth component we propose to identify is the power of ideas, rational or ethical.[2]

In any one country all these forms of power will be discreetly or openly present, although the most potent, over time, is of course the last, the power of ideas. But what is the manner by which the more acceptable of these forms of power can be harnessed and used? The following is the view from the vantage of regional and local planning:

'What' information about resources and ecology.... and		*Power systems* involving decision taking and governance... and
'Why' information of human aspirations and forces.... and	...applied in the agreed development model to...	
'How' information of techniques for development....		*Resources* involving all those that are renewable, non-renewable and extrinsic

Thus, operationally, ecodevelopment is concerned with the gathering of 'what', 'why' and 'how' information as a prelude to the process whereby the power available to a society is applied as a physical moment to resources. The component in all this which must be firmly established is, of course, the ecodevelopment ideal.

New internal order

After the depression of the 1930s there emerged a 'New Deal' predicated, in Haq's words, on the principle that 'every dollar going to labour was not a dollar taken away from profits but would come back twice over through effective demand and really grease the wheels of prosperity'.[3] This constituted the capitalist response to a problem experienced from a position of relative wealth. Of course, the depression affected poorer nations, but relatively less than it affected the rich (its worst consequences did not compare, for example, to the post-depression Bengal famines induced by physically enforced interventions). However, the economic conditions of the 1930s do not exist now in either the overdeveloped or the low income countries and calling for a 'new new deal', in the form of a New Economic International Order, to solve 'todays' economic problems—more particularly those of the heavily populated poor countries—is futile; for aside from an increase in the 'generosity' of aid flows by a mere decimal point or two, the poorer countries receive little now, and can expect less *per capita* in future from the Northern nations. Given this situation what they can do is work out a new internal order for themselves, nation by nation yet sharing experiences, each nation planning in accordance with its resource capability.

Fulfilling 'basic needs' is essential to any policy for a new internal order. The call is to meet basic guarantees in nutrition, clothing and shelter, plus access to medical care and basic education. There is nothing new here; the re-expression is intended to emphasise the elements in a new internal order.

Fundamental though the list may seem, however, it can only be fulfilled through political commitment and sound administration. This is vital, although accountability to people and parliament is also important. Education and relevant research are also key elements. Ultimately, however, responsibility rests with politicians, senior civil servants and academics to work out how the redistributive objectives underlying the fulfilment of basic guarantees through ecodevelopment can be sustained without lowering *per capita* product or creating any additional hardship or environmental disequilibrium.

The aim in the longer term is to move beyond basic guarantees by increasing capital stocks and consumption of consumer durables in a manner that remains consistent with the principles of ecodevelopment. This introduces additional options; whether to have incentive schemes, social services for the aged and infirm, communications for social purposes, equal pay for equal work, population limitation, technological reforms and land reform. A complete list of new options would be longer, but whatever is added to it the overall aim is economic equity, social harmony and environmental balance in pursuit of overall human advance.

External reinforcement

Most low income countries strive towards self-sufficiency but all of them have to live in a trading relationship which operates to the advantage of the already wealthy countries and which they cannot easily do without. It is a situation in which increases in trade are only gained at the expense of an ever widening disparity between low and high income countries. Reconciling the opposing aims of ever increasing self-reliance within a framework of international dependency requires that low income countries maintain and improve some of their external linkages.

Among the improvements which they can support is, first and foremost, the drawing up of improved producers' commodity agreements, giving low income countries a fairer deal and high income countries the opportunity to participate credibly to adjust disparities in trading relationships. A second, ancilliary and less beneficial measure which low income countries can adopt is to endorse the setting up of a common fund even though this may be only $6 to $10 billion. Thirdly, poorer nations must ensure that their voice is heard at international fora, and is felt threat by voting in concert—which in turn requires communication between low income countries on the basis of coalitions which lend additional support to their aspirations. Fourth, control of common property resources, a matter usually treated as less significant for poorer countries but of vital concern to humanity as a whole, provides an opportunity for them to act responsibly and be seen to do so (at little extra cost to themselves) whilst encouraging others to do likewise. Lastly, low income countries can offer a peace brokerage service operated with self-interest in mind—namely, to get some of the extravagant arms expenditure in richer nations siphoned off as aid, whilst cutting down on their own domestic arms expenditure.

The task, at least is clear:

1 Substitute the reality of local human improvement (progress) for the notion of national economic growth.

2 Strive always to advance social wellbeing along with the material quality of life.

3 Use non-renewable resources thoughtfully.

4 Conserve as though for the rest of human history those resources that are renewable.

In a phrase: follow the ideal of ecodevelopment action with its *national* emphasis upon economic equity, social harmony and environmental balance in the *local* pursuit of individual fulfilment, household self-sufficiency and community self-reliance.

Notes

1 I.G. Simmons, *The Ecology of Natural Resources,* Edward Arnold, London, 1974, p.370.

2 Jan Tinbergen (co-ordinator), *Reshaping the International Order,* Hutchinson, London, 1977, p.7.

3 Mahbub ul Haq, *The Poverty Curtain,* Columbia University Press, New York, 1976, p.173.

4 This is also the aim of the Haq and Tinbergen reports, ibid.

Appendix

Eight Point Development Plan —
Government of Papua New Guinea

1 A rapid increase in the proportion of the economy under the control of Papua New Guinea individuals and groups and in the proportion of personal and property income that goes to Papua New Guineans.

2 More equal distribution of economic benefits, including movement towards equalisation of incomes among people and towards equalisation of services among different areas of the country.

3 Decentralisation of economic activity, planning and government spending, with emphasis on agricultural development, village industry, better internal trade and more spending channelled to local and area bodies.

4 An emphasis on small scale artisan, service and business activity, relying where possible on typically Papua New Guinean forms of economic organisation.

5 A more self-reliant economy, less dependent for its needs on imported goods and services and better able to meet the needs of its people through local production.

6 An increasing capacity for meeting government spending needs from locally raised revenue.

7 A rapid increase in the equal and active participation of women in all forms of economic and social activity.

8 Government control and involvement in those sectors of the economy where control is necessary to achieve the desired kind of development.

Bibliography

The objective with this bibliography has been to set down the texts made available in English during the 1970 decade provided they relate usefully to development planning, resource conservation and environmental protection.

Alonso, William, 'Urban Zero Population Growth' (1973): *The No-growth Society,* published by Daedalus, special issue, Fall 1973.

Amin, Samir, *Neo-Colonialism in West Africa,* Penguin African Library, London, 1973.

'Accumulation and Development—A Theoretical Model', *Review of African Political Economy,* no.1, August 1974.

Andreski, Stanislav, *Social Science as Sorcery,* Andre Deutsch, 1972.

Aziz, Sartai, *Rural Development: Learning from China,* Macmillan, London, 1978.

Bain, Joe S., *Environmental Decay,* Little Brown, Boston, 1973.

Barnett, Andy H. and Yandle, Bruce, 'Allocating Environmental Resources', *Public Finance,* vol.28, no.1, 1973, pp.11-9.

Baumgart, I.L. and Datson, Patricia J., 'Environmental Protection and Enhancement Procedures', *New Zealand Science Review,* vol.31, no.3, 1974.

Bennett, John W., Hesegawa, Sukehiro and Levine Solomon B., 'Japan', *Environment,* vol.XV, no.10, December 1973, pp.6-13.

Birch, J.W., 'Geography and Resource Management', *Journal of Environmental Management,* vol.I, no.1, 1973, pp.3-11.

Biswas, Asit K., *Energy and the Environment,* Information Canada Catalogue, No En, 36-509/1, Ottawa, 1974.

Boucher, K., Harris, N., *Environmental Research Register,* African Environment Special Report 4, International African Institute, London, 1977.

Boulding, Kenneth E., 'The Shadow of the Stationary State', *The No-Growth Society,* published by Daedalus, special issue, Fall 1973.

Boyle, G., *Living on the Sun,* Calder and Boyars, London, 1975.

Broadbent, K.P., 'The Transformation of Chinese Agriculture and its Effects on the Environment', *International Relations,* vol.4, no.1, 1972.

Brookfield, Harold, *Interdependent Development,* Methuen, London, 1975.

Brooks, Harvey, 'The Technology of Zero Growth', *The No-Growth Society,* published by Daedalus, special issue, Fall 1973.

Brooks, Harvey and Bowers, Raymond, 'The Assessment of Technology', *Scientific American,* vol.222, no.2, February 1970.

Brown, Lester R. and Eckholm, Erik P., *By Bread Alone,* Praegar, New York, 1974.

Brown, Michael B., *The Economics of Imperialism,* Penguin, London, 1974.

Burch, William R. (ed), *Readings in Ecology, Energy and Human Society,* Harper and Row, New York, 1977.

Burchell, Robert W. and Listokin, David, *The Environmental Impact Handbook,* Centre for Urban Policy Research, New Brunswick, 1975.

Carter, Vernon Gill and Dale, Tom, *Topsoil and Civilization,* revised edition, University of Oklahoma Press, 1974.

Chadwick, G.F., *A Systems View of Planning,* Pergammon Press, London 1971.

Chang Hung, 'Water Pollution and its Control in Singapore', *Towards a Clean and Healthy Environment,* Ministry of the Environment, Singapore, 1973.

Chan Kai Lok and Associates, 'Mosquito Free Campaign', *Towards a Clean and Healthy Environment,* Ministry of the Environment, Singapore, 1973.

Chapman, Peter, *Energy Options for Britain,* Penguin Special, London, 1975.

Chua Yong Hai, 'Air Pollution Control in Singapore', *Towards a Clean and Healthy Environment,* Ministry of the Environment, Singapore, 1973.

Chughtai, M.I.D., *Nutrition and National Development,* Proceedings of the First Commonwealth Conference on Development and Human Ecology, Malta, 1970, Charles Knight, London, 1972, pp.150-5.

Clark, C., *Population Growth and Land Use,* Macmillan, London, 1977.

Cloud, Preston, 'This Finite Earth', *Arts and Science Review,* Spring 1971, Indiana University, pp.17-32.

Cloudsley-Thompson, J.J., *Terrestrial Environment,* Croomhelm, London 1975.

Coates, B.E., Johnston, R.J. and Knox, P.L., *Geography and Inequality,* Oxford University Press, 1977.

Cole, H.S.D., Christopher Freeman, Marie Jahoda and K.L.R. Pavitt, 'The Structure of the World Models', *Thinking about the Future: A Critique of the Limits to Growth,* Chatto and Windus, London, 1973.

Commission for the Environment, New Zealand, *Environmental Protection and Enhancement Procedures,* Government Printer, Wellington, 1973.

Commoner, Barry, *The Closing Circle: Confronting the Environmental Crisis,* Johnathon Cape, London, 1972.

Commoner, Barry, Corr, Michael and Stamler, Paul J., 'The Causes of Pollution', *Environment,* vol.XIII, no.3, April 1971, pp.2-19.

Cooke, R.U. and Doornkamp, J.C., *Geomorphology in Environmental Management,* Clarendon Press, Oxford, 1974.

Cottrell, A., *Environmental Economics,* Edward Arnold, London, 1978.

Dansereau, Pierre, *The Human Predicament,* Proceedings of the First Commonwealth Conference on Development and Human Ecology, Malta, 1970, Charles Knight, London, 1972, pp.1-39.

Dasmann, Raymond, *Environmental Conservation,* (third edition), Wiley, New York, 1972.

Davis, Kingsley, 'Zero Population Growth', *The No-Growth Society,* published in Daedalus (special issue) Fall 1973.

Denman, D.R., *Institutional Factors in Environmental Control,* Proceedings of the First Commonwealth Conference on Development and Human Ecology, Malta, 1970. Charles Knight, London, 1972, pp.42-50.

Department of Energy, United Kingdom, *Energy Saving in Industry,* Central Office of Information, 1975.

Dickinson, H. and Winnington, T.L., 'Examples of Rural Technology from China', School of Engineering Sciences, University of Edinburgh, 1974 (mimeographed).

Dickson, David, *Alternative Technology: and the Politics of Technical Change,* Fontana/Collins, Glasgow, 1974.

Dickson, Edward M., 'Recycling Used Energy', *Environment,* vol.XIV, no.6, July/August 1972, pp.36-41.

Donaldson, Peter, *Worlds Apart: The Economic Gulf Between Nations,* Pelican, London, 1973.

Dove, J., Miriung, T. and Togolo, M., 'Mining Bitterness', in *Problems of Choice,* Peter G. Sack (ed), Australian National University Press, Canberra, 1974.

Dunn, P.D., *Appropriate Technology,* Macmillan, London, 1978.

Eckholm, Erik P., 'Desertification: A World Problem', *Ambio,* vol.IV, no.4, 1975.
Losing Ground, Morton, New York, 1976.
Editors of *The Ecologist,* 'A Blueprint for Survival', Penguin Special, 1972.
Editors of *Scientific American,* 'The Biosphere', W.H. Freeman, San Francisco, 1970.
'Energy and Power', W.H. Freeman, San Francisco, 1971.
Ehrlich, P.R., Ehrlich, A.H. and Holdren, J.P., *Ecoscience. Population, Resources and Environment,* W.H. Freeman, San Francisco, 1977.
Enzensburger, Hans Magnus, 'A Critique of Political Ecology', in Hilary Rose and Steven Rose (eds) *The Political Economy of Science,* Macmillan, London, 1976.

Farvar, Taghi, Thomas, Margaret L., Boksenbaum, Howard and Soule, Theodore N., 'The Pollution of Asia', *Environment,* vol.XIII, no.8, October 1971, pp.10-17.
Foley, Gerald, *The Energy Question,* Penguin Books, London, 1976.
'Energy Resources in a Planning Context', *Built Environment,* July 1972, pp.271-3.
Freeman, Christopher, H.S.D. Cole, Mari Jahoda, K.L.R. Pavitt, 'Malthus with a Computer', *Thinking about the Future: A Critique of the Limits to Growth,* Chatto and Windus, London, 1973.
Fuglesang, Andreas, *Doing Things Together,* Dag Hammarskjold Foundation, Uppsala, 1977.

Garcia, Richard, 'The Control of Malaria', *Environment,* vol.XIV, no.5, June 1972, pp.2-9.
Gates, David M., 'The Flow of Energy in the Biosphere', *Scientific American,* vol.225, no.3, September 1971.
Geertz, Clifford, *Agricultural Induction: The Processes of Ecological Change in Indonesia,* University of California Press, Berkeley, 1971.
Geoffrey, K.A., *Development and Underdevelopment: A Marxist Analysis,* Macmillan, London, 1975.
Geological Survey, United States, *A Procedure for Evaluating Environmental Impact,* prepared by Luna B. Leopold, Frank E. Clarke, Bruce B. Hanshaw and James R. Balsey, Circular 645, Washington, 1971.
Georgescu-Roegen, Nicholas, *Energy and Economic Myths,* Pergammon, 1977.
Gilpin, Alan, *Dictionary of Economic Terms,* Butterworths, London, 1977.
Glacken, Clarence, J., *Traces on the Rhodian Shore,* University of California Press, Los Angeles, 1977.

Glantz, Michael H. (ed), *The Politics of Natural Disaster*, Praeger, New York, 1975.

Glikson, Artur, *The Ecological Basis of Planning*, Martinus Nijhoff, The Hague, 1971.

Goodland, R.J.A. and Irwin, H.S., *Amazon Jungle: Green Hell to Arid Desert*, Elsevier, Amsterdam, 1975.

Grayson, Melvin, J. and Shepard, Thomas R., *The Disaster Lobby*, Follet, Chicago, 1973.

Great Britain, Cabinet Office, *Future World Trends*, a discussion paper on world trends in population, resources, pollution and their implications, HMSO, London, 1976.

Grenfell, Julian, *Development and Ecology*, Proceedings of the First Commonwealth Conference on Development and Human Ecology, Malta, 1970. Charles Knight, London, 1972, pp.179-83.

Haggett, Peter, *Geography: A Modern Synthesis*, Harper and Row, New York, 1972.

Haq, Mahbub ul, *The Poverty Curtain*, Columbia University Press, New York, 1976.

Hirst, Eric, 'The Energy Cost of Pollution Control', *Environment*, vol. XV, no.8, October 1973, pp.16-34.

Hjalte, K., Lidgren, K. and Stahl, I., *Environmental Policy and Welfare Economics*, Cambridge University Press, Cambridge, 1977.

Holdgate, M.W. and Woodman, M.J., 'Ecology and Planning', *Bulletin of the British Ecological Society*, vol.VI, no.4, 1976.

Holister, Geoffrey and Porteous, Andrew, *The Environment: A Dictionary of the World About Us*, Arrow Books, London, 1976.

Hubbert, M. King, 'The Energy Resources of the Earth', *Scientific American*, vol.225, no.3, September 1971.

Hutchings, B., Forrester, A., Jain, R.K. and Balbach, Harold, *Environmental Impact Analysis: Current Methodologies and Future Directions*, University of Illinois, 1976.

Hutchinson, Sir Joseph, *The Challenge of the Third World*, Cambridge University Press, Cambridge, 1975.

Idyll, Clarence P., 'The Anchovy Crisis', *Scientific American*, vol.228, no.6, June 1973.

Isard, Walter, Chognill, C.L., Kissin, J., Seyforth, R.H. and Tatlock, R., *Ecologic-Economic Analysis for Regional Development*, Free Press, New York, 1972.

Jackson, I.J., *Climate, Water and Agriculture in the Tropics*, Longman, London, 1977.

Jacoby, E.H., *Man and Land*, Andre Deutsch, London, 1971.

Jalee, Pierre, *The Pillage of the Third World*, Modern Reader, New York, 1970.

Jeffers, J.N.R., 'Systems Modelling and Analysis in Resource Management', *Journal of Environmental Management,* vol.1, no.1, 1973, pp.13-28.

Johnson, D. Gale, *World Agriculture in Disarray,* Fontana/Collins, London, 1973.

Johnson, Harry G., *Man and his Environment,* published by the British-North America Committee, May 1973.

Johnson, Willard R., 'Should the Poor Buy No Growth?' *The No-Growth Society,* published by Daedalus (special issue) Fall 1973.

Kapp, K. William, *The Social Costs of Private Enterprise,* Schocken Books, New York, 1971.

Klotz, John W., *Ecology Crisis: God's Creation and Man's Pollution,* Concordia Press, London, 1972.

Kneese, Allen V., *Economics and Environment,* Penguin Books, London 1977.

Kneese, Allen V., Rolfe, Sidney E., Harned, Joseph W., *Managing the Environment,* Praeger, New York, 1971.

Kneese, Allen, V. and Schultze, Charles L., *Pollution Prices and Public Policy,* Brookings Institute, Washington, 1975.

Koenigsberger, Otto H., Bernstein, Beverley, et.al., *Infrastructural Problems of the Cities of the Developing Countries,* an International Urbanisation Survey funded by the Ford Foundation, July 1971.

Koh Thong Sam and Yap Kim Seng, 'Control of the Litter Problem in Singapore', *Towards a Clean and Healthy Environment,* Ministry of the Environment, Singapore, 1973.

Leach, Gerald, *Energy and Food Production,* International Institute for Environment and Development, 1976.

'Net Energy Analysis—Is it any Use?' *Energy Policy,* December 1975.

Lean, Geoffrey, *Rich World, Poor World,* Allen and Unwin, London, 1978.

Lipton, M., *Why Poor People Stay Poor,* Temple Smith, London, 1977.

Lovins, Amory B., *Soft Energy Paths,* Ballinger, New York, 1977.

Lye Thim Fatt, 'The Refuse Disposal Aspects of Solid Wastes Management in Singapore', *Towards a Clean and Healthy Environment,* Ministry of the Environment, Singapore, 1973.

McHarg, Ian L., *Design with Nature,* Doubleday, New York, 1971.

McKean, Roland N., 'Growth Versus No Growth: An Evaluation', *The No-Growth Society,* published by Daedalus (special issue) Fall 1973.

Makhijani, Arjun, *Energy and Agriculture in the Third World,* Ballinger, Cambridge, Mass., 1975.

Energy Policy for the Rural Third World, International Institute for Environment and Development, 1976.

Matthews, William H., 'Objective and Subjective Judgements in Environmental Impact Analysis', *Environmental Conservation*, vol.2, nos.2-3, Lausanne, 1975.

Macbean, A. and Balasubramanyon, V.N., *Meeting the Third World Challenge*, Macmillan, London, 1976.

Meadows, Donella H., Meadows, Dennis L., Randers, Jorgen and Behrans, William W., *The Limits to Growth*, Earth Island, London, 1972.

Meier, Gerald M., *Problems of Cooperation for Development*, Oxford University Press, New York, 1974.

Miller, G. Tyler, *Replenish the Earth*, Wadsworth Press, California, 1972.

Mishan, E.J., *The Economic Growth Debate*, Allen and Unwin, London, 1976.

The Costs of Economic Growth, Penguin Books, London (reprinted 1973).

'The Wages of Growth', *The No-Growth Society*, published by Daedalus (special issue) Fall 1973.

Momis, J., 'Taming the Dragon', *Problems of Choice*, Peter G. Sack (ed), Australian National University Press, Canberra, 1974.

Mumford, Lewis, *Findings and Keepings*, Secker and Warburg, New York, 1975.

Nelson, Michael, *The Development of Tropical Lands: Policy Issues in Latin America*, John Hopkins University Press, 1973.

Newell, Reginald E., 'The Global Circulation of Atmospheric Pollution', *Scientific American*, vol.224, no.1, January 1971.

Nicholson, Max, *The Environmental Revolution*, Hodder and Stoughton, London, 1970.

Odum, Eugene P., *Fundamentals of Ecology*, (3rd edition), Saunders, Philadelphia, 1971.

OECD, *Economic Measurement of Environmental Damage*, OECD, Paris, 1976.

Problems of Environmental Economics, Record of a Seminar, Summer 1971, OECD, Paris, 1972.

The Polluter Pays Principle, OECD, Paris, 1975.

Problems in Transfrontier Pollution, OECD, Paris, 1974.

Office of Environment and Conservation, Government of Papua New Guinea, *The National Goals*, Port Moresby, 1975.

Onyemelukwe, C.C., *Economic Underdevelopment: An Inside View*, Longman Group, London, 1974.

Paine, Suzanne, 'Balanced Development: Maoist Conception and Chinese Practice', *World Development*, vol.4, no.4, Pergammon Press, London, 1976.

Paterson, J.H., *Land, Work and Resources,* Edward Arnold, London, 1972.

Paxton, Jonijane, *An Experiment in Ecology: AMAZ Henderson,* Mountain Empire Publishing, Denver, 1974.

Payer, Cheryl, *The Debt Trap: The IMF and the Third World,* Penguin Books, London, 1974.

Peterson, F.M. and Fisher, A.C., 'The Exploitation of Extractive Resources', *The Economic Journal,* vol.87, December 1977, pp.681-721.

Pinchet, Gifford, 'Marine Farming', *Scientific American,* vol.223, no.6, December 1970.

Poore, M.E.D., 'Ecology and Conservation in Land Use', *Chartered Surveyor,* November 1972, pp.216-8.

Porteous, Andrew, *Maintaining the Environment,* Open University Press, London, 1972.

Potter, Van Rensellaer, *Bioethics: Bridge to the Future,* Prentice Hall, Englewood Cliffs, 1971.

Quick, Horace F., *Population Ecology,* Pegasus, London, 1974.

Qurashi, M.M., *Project Selection and Transfer of Technology,* Proceedings of the Pakistan Academy of Science, vol.II, no.2, 1974, pp.9-18. *The Appropriateness of Technology Transferred,* Appropriate Technology Development Organisation, 1977, p.13 (mimeographed).

Ramsay, William and Anderson, Claude, *Managing the Environment: An Economic Primer,* Macmillan, London, 1972.

Rappaport, Roy A., 'The Flow of Energy in an Agricultural Society', *Scientific American,* vol.225, no.3, September 1971.

Resources for the Future, *Environmental Matrix: A Conceptual Tool to Unravel the Environmental Tangle,* RFF Reprint no.107, Washington, February 1973.

Robinson, J., *Freedom and Necessity,* Allen and Unwin, London, 1970.

Rodney, Walter, *How Europe Underdeveloped Africa,* Bougle L'Ouverture, and Dar es Salaam: Tanzania Publishing House, London, 1972.

Rowley, Charles K., *Pollution and Public Policy,* Inaugural Lecture, Newcastle University, 1975.

Sack, Peter G. (ed), *Problem of Choice: Land in Papua New Guinea's Future,* Australian National University Press, Canberra, 1974.

Sahlins, Marshall, 'The Original Affluent Society', *The Ecologist,* vol.IV, no.5, June 1974, pp.181-9.

Samuel, F.J. and Ang, Lawrence, 'Environmental Health Laws and Enforcement', *Towards a Clean and Healthy Environment,* Ministry of the Environment, Singapore, 1973.

Savage, D.T., Burke, M., Coupe, J.D., Duchesnean, T.D., Wihry, D.F. and Wilson, J.A., *Economics of Environmental Improvement,* Houghton Miflin, Boston, 1974.

Schofield, S., *Development and the Problem of Village Nutrition*, Groom Helm, London, 1979.

Schumacher, E.G., *Small is Beautiful: A Study of Economics as if People Mattered*, Abacus, London, 1974.

Scorer, R.S., *The Clever Moron*, Routledge and Kegan Paul, London, 1977.

Scott, J.C., *The Moral Economy of the Peasant*, Yale University Press, 1977.

Seneca, Joseph J. and Tansigg, Michael K., *Environmental Economics*, Prentice Hall, New Jersey, 1979.

Sewell, W.R. Derrick, 'Broadening the Approach to Evaluation of Resources Management and Decision Making', *Journal of Environmental Management*, vol.1, no.1, 1973, pp.33-63.

Simmons, I.G., *The Ecology of Natural Resources*, Edward Arnold, London, 1974.

Singh, Marindar, *Economics—The Crisis of Ecology*, Oxford University Press, Delhi, 1976.

Skinner, David N., 'Ecology in Planning', *Planning Outlook*, vol.12 (new series) Spring 1972.

Smith, Nigel, *Brazil's Transamazon Highway Settlement Scheme*, Proceedings of the Association of American Geographers, vol.8, Los Angeles, 1976.

Stahler, Arthur N. and Stahler, Alan H., *Environmental Geoscience: Interaction Between Natural Systems and Man*, Hamilton, Santa Barbara, 1973.

Stewart, Francis, *Technology and Underdevelopment*, Macmillan, London, 1978.

'Technology and Underdevelopment', *ODI Review*, no.1, 1977.

Stretton, Hugh, *Capitalism, Socialism and the Environment*, Cambridge University Press, London, 1976.

Summers, Claude M., 'The Conversion of Energy', *Scientific American*, vol.225, no.3, September 1971.

Tamplin, Arthur R., 'Solar Energy', *Environment*, vol.XV, no.5, June 1973, pp.16-34.

Task Force on Human Settlements, Philippines. 'The Ecosystem Approach to Human Settlement Planning' (TFHS/B/H/DRZ/510), Quezon City, December 1975 (mimeographed).

Teller, Aaron J., 'Ecosystem Technology: Theory and Practice', *American Institute of Chemical Engineers*, vol.9, no.70, 1974.

Tinbergen, Jan (co-ordinator), *Reshaping the International Order*, Hutchinson, London, 1977.

Trudge, C., *The Famine Business*, Faber, London, 1977.

Turnham, David (assisted by Ingelies Jaeger), *The Employment Problem in Less Developed Countries*, OECD Development Centre, Paris, 1971.

Ward, Barbara, *The Home of Man,* Penguin Books, London, 1976.

Ward, Barbara and Dubos, Rene, *Only One Earth: The Care and Mainte-nance of a Small Planet,* Penguin/Andre Deutsch, London, 1972.

White, Lynn, 'The Historical Roots of our Ecological Crisis', in *Politics and Environment,* Walt Anderson (ed), Goodyear, Pacific Palisades, California, 1970.

Widstrand, Carl G., 'The Rationale of Nomad Economy', *Ambio,* vol.IV, no.4, 1975.

Wilkes, H. Garrison and Wilkes, Susan, 'The Green Revolution', *Environment,* vol.IV, no.8, October 1972, pp.32-9.

Woods, Barbara (ed), *Eco-Solutions: A Casebook for the Environmental Crisis,* Schonkman, Cambridge, Mass., 1972.

Woodwell, George M., 'The Energy Cycle of the Biosphere', *Scientific American,* vol.223, no.3, September 1976.

World Bank Group, *Environment and Development,* World Bank, Washington, 1975.

World Health Organisation, *Appraisal of the Hygenic Quality of Housing and its Environment,* Report (no.353) of a WHO Export Committee. World Health Organisation, Geneva, 1967.

Worthington, E. Barton, *Cooperation in Ecology,* Proceedings of the First Commonwealth Conference on Development and Human Ecology, Malta, 1970. Charles Knight, London, 1972, pp.184-9.

Zeckhauser, Richard, 'The Risks of Growth', *The No-Growth Society,* published by Daedalus (special issue) Fall 1973.

Index

with Corr, Michael and Stamler, Paul, 100, 165
Cottrell, Sir Alan, 43
Cuba, 107

Dansereau, Pierre, 99
DDT, 43, 44
development:
  concept of, 1, 4—5
  defined, 90
  economics of, 139—142, 143
  extant systems, 85, 90—3
  external diseconomies of, 151—8
  'fashions' in, 97—8
  'goods' and 'bads' in, 120—1, 124—5
  Marxist view, 92
  modelling environmental component in, 99—104
  incomes, 147
  policies, 96—8
  system, 86—7
  vision of society and, 104
disasters, natural and human, 188—9
disease:
  misery of and cure, 9, 12
  nutrition correlated, 63—4
Dorner, Peter, 146

Eckholm, Erik, 19
ecodevelopment, 1, 107
  and material consumption North and South, 8
  concern with resources, 45
  dealing with large projects, 184—6
  guidelines to, 113—4, 196
  ideals of, 110
  need for political will to implement, 177—8
  past and present concern with, 10—11
  philosophy of, 108—11, 199

planning for. See also environmental planning
  policies for low income areas, 91, 98
  principles, 8—9, 12—14, 111—12, 196
  relation to power, 197
  social justice and, 110
ecosystems, 31, 36—7, 40
  absorption type, 40, 41, 42
  aliveness of, 36—7
  classified, 40—4
  composite type, 41, 42
  global, 46
  in harmony with others, 40
  natural type, 41, 42—3
  production type, 41, 42
  reciprocation within themselves, 37, 40
  technology and, 163
Ehrlich, P.R. and A.H., and Holdren, J.R., 100
employment, 133:
  effect of new technology on, 168—9
  methods of decentralising, 135
  rural out-migration, 134—6
  urban, 133—4
energy accounting, 189,190
environment:
  effect of expanding population on, 44—5
  effects of waste disposal, 43—4, 156, 157
  environmental goals, 94—5
  protection of, 13
environmental planning:
  impact assessment (EIA), 189—190
  operational management, 182—4
  planning apparatus, 180—2
  planning networks, 179—84
  regulative apparatus, 182

214

217

undernourishment in, 63

underdevelopment:
  relation with overdevelopment,
  4—5
UNCTAD, 6, 79
UNESCO, 96
United Nations:
  demographic data, 2
  Environmental Programme
  (UNEP), 26, 96
United States of America:
  Department of Agriculture, 72
  growth and its effects, 126—8
  'New Deal', 198
  rice growing compared with
  China, 64
urban areas, 73—4, 78
  defining, 73
  development of, 73—4
  dwelling size and rates of
  occupancy, 76—7
  need to clean up squalor, 12—
  13
  Northern development of, 91
  precincts in, 78
  subsistance urbanisation, 74
  urban—rural antimonies, 109—
  10

Volta river project, 29

Ward, Barbara and Dubos, René,
  45, 128
  approaches to ecodevelopment
  109
waste disposal:
  effect on environment, 43—4,
  156, 157
  in mining, 156, 186
water:
  open water exploitation, 188
  problems caused by irrigation,
  29, 103
  resource depletion, 28—9
whales, 26
wheat, 71
  world grain trade, 72
Woodruff, W., 49
world:
  deserts, 26
  economic classification of 100
  countries, 140—1
  energy and income, 20—1
  North and South, 2, 79
  North—South trading relation,
  6—7, 79, 142, 143, 199
  Northern prosperity and
  Southern denial, 5, 52, 95—6
  population, 3. See also separate entry
  problems of rich nations, 195

Zambia, 107

E6